# How to Revise
## for A-Level

## Revise your A-Level revision strategy with CGP!

So you've made it to sixth form. The grass is green, the sun is shining and GCSEs are a distant memory. Try not to get too relaxed though — there are A-Levels on the horizon...

Happily, this CGP book will help you power through anything your courses can throw at you. It's packed with expert advice on everything from choosing your subjects to acing your last exam.

With specific advice for all the major A-Level subjects, plus useful write-in timetables and planners for your revision, it'll be sunshine and rainbows again before you know it.

# Contents

Published by CGP

*Editors:*
Siân Butler, Andy Cashmore, Robbie Driscoll, Sean Walsh

*Contributors:*
Encarna Aparicio-Dominguez, Ben Armstrong, Lauren Burns,
Charlotte Cairns, Barrie Crowther, Mark Edwards, Paul Garrett,
Alice Kirby, David Martindill, Victoria Skelton, Brenda Turnbull

With thanks to Claire Boulter and Matthew Sims for the proofreading.
With thanks to Emily Smith for the copyright research.

Photo on p 39 © Patrik Giardino/ Stone/ Getty Images

ISBN: 978 1 78908 627 0   Printed by Elanders Ltd, Newcastle upon Tyne.

Clipart from Corel®
Based on the classic CGP style created by Richard Parsons.

Text, design, layout and original illustrations © Coordination Group Publications Ltd. (CGP) 2020
All rights reserved.

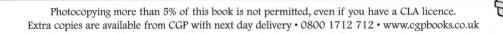

# How To Use This Book

Moving from GCSEs to A-Levels can seem a bit overwhelming, but this book is full of information and advice to help you stay afloat. First up is a quick overview of what's covered in each section of this book.

## Here's What to Expect in Each Section

You don't necessarily have to read the book in this order — feel free to jump around to any bits that are particularly relevant at the time.

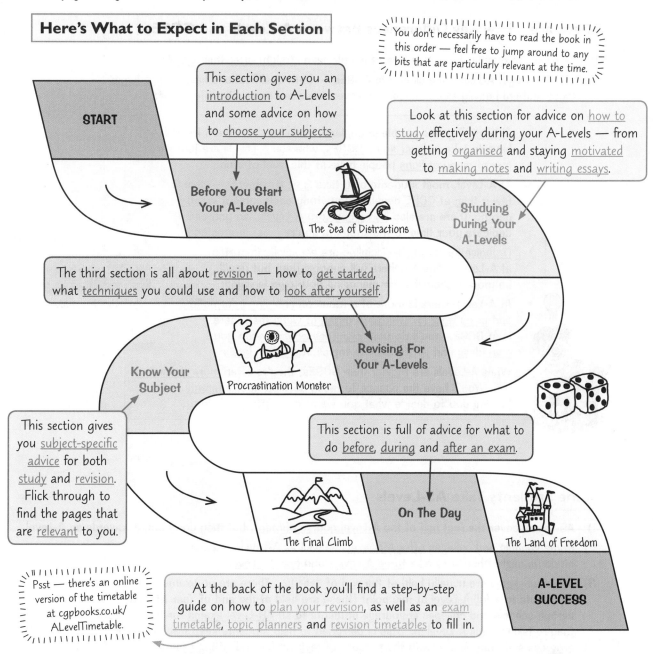

This section gives you an introduction to A-Levels and some advice on how to choose your subjects.

Look at this section for advice on how to study effectively during your A-Levels — from getting organised and staying motivated to making notes and writing essays.

The third section is all about revision — how to get started, what techniques you could use and how to look after yourself.

This section gives you subject-specific advice for both study and revision. Flick through to find the pages that are relevant to you.

This section is full of advice for what to do before, during and after an exam.

Psst — there's an online version of the timetable at cgpbooks.co.uk/ALevelTimetable.

At the back of the book you'll find a step-by-step guide on how to plan your revision, as well as an exam timetable, topic planners and revision timetables to fill in.

**START**

**Before You Start Your A-Levels**

The Sea of Distractions

**Studying During Your A-Levels**

**Know Your Subject**

Procrastination Monster

**Revising For Your A-Levels**

**The Final Climb**

**On The Day**

The Land of Freedom

**A-LEVEL SUCCESS**

## Top tip — don't try using the book this way up...

Even if some of these sections don't seem relevant to you right now (e.g. if you won't be starting revision for a while), it might still be helpful to have a skim through the whole book to get you thinking about what's to come.

# Introduction to A-Levels

A-Level stands for 'Advanced Level', but while it's easy to assume that A-Levels are just tougher versions of GCSEs, there's a bit more to them. Here's a quick overview of how taking A-Levels is a different experience.

## There are a Few Key Differences Between A-Levels and GCSEs

1) A-Levels are qualifications that lots of people take straight after their GCSEs.

2) In some ways, A-Levels are similar to GCSEs — both qualifications have an academic focus and are heavily exam-based. However, there are some big differences:

- Almost all young people in England, Wales and Northern Ireland have to take at least some GCSEs, whereas A-Levels are just one of many options people have at this level of study.

- At A-Level, most students only take 3 or 4 subjects — this is fewer than at GCSE because you study each subject in more depth. There are also no compulsory A-Levels, so you can dedicate your time to the subjects you're most interested in.

- Organisation and self-discipline are especially important at A-Level. Your teachers will support you, but you'll be more responsible for managing your own learning.

- At A-Level, there is more of a focus on applying information and using your knowledge in different ways than there is at GCSE. You'll do your own research, develop your own ideas and get to explore topics in greater detail.

- While A-Levels are trickier than GCSEs, they're often more rewarding too. You'll have the chance to really develop your interests, helping you to decide what you want to do after sixth form.

Lily found that studying things in more depth came with its own challenges.

## Some Students Take AS-Levels

1) AS-Levels cover the first half of the A-Level course content, but they don't count towards an A-Level.

2) Some schools and colleges offer AS-Levels as well as A-Levels, so some students might choose to take three A-Levels and one AS-Level.

3) AS-Level exams are usually held at the end of Year 12. There are no exams that contribute to a full A-Level at this point (these are held at the end of Year 13), but certain schools and colleges encourage students to sit AS-Level exams for the subjects they're taking a full A-Level in. This is designed to help students keep track of their progress and stay familiar with the process of revising for and sitting exams.

4) Don't worry too much if you're not taking AS-Levels or if your school or college doesn't offer them. Universities and employers understand that schools and colleges have different approaches to them.

# Where to Study Your A-Levels

It's not just the academic stuff that's different at A-Level. Your student experience is likely to change too...

## There are Several Places you Can Take A-Levels

Secondary School Sixth Form

If your secondary school has a sixth form, you could stay at the same school. Otherwise, you could move to another.

Sixth Form College or Further Education College

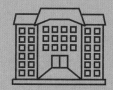

Some people choose to study at a college designed for students aged 16-18.

At Home

Some people choose to study their A-Levels at home (this is more common with international and mature students).

## Things are a Bit Different During Sixth Form

Sixth form is a stepping stone between school and university — this means your experience of sixth form may be a bit different from school:

- Lots of sixth forms have a more relaxed atmosphere than you might be used to. Some schools have common rooms and a more relaxed uniform for sixth form students, while at many colleges there's no uniform and you can call teachers by their first names.

- A lot of sixth forms encourage you to do some form of recreational activity on a regular basis. There's often a big range of clubs and societies available to sixth formers, particularly at colleges.

- Your timetable is likely to look different, as you'll have more lessons for each subject.

- You might have free periods. These are timetabled sessions when you don't have a lesson and can focus on independent study (see pages 14-15). In sixth form, you'll be expected to motivate yourself and be responsible for your own time, so it's up to you to use free periods effectively.

Although he no longer had a uniform, Ted never forgot to wear his thinking cap.

## The Year 11 rugby captain quit last year. He's now the *sixth* former captain...

If you're doing A-Levels, it's (hopefully) because you've decided that it's what you want to do. This is one reason why the atmosphere in sixth form is often more relaxed — people are doing subjects they're really interested in.

# Choosing Your A-Levels

There are a lot of A-Levels to choose from, so it's worth taking the time to research your options thoroughly.

## Think About These Questions When Choosing Your Subjects...

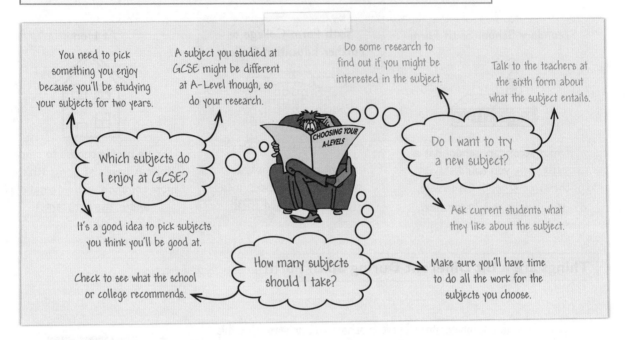

You need to pick something you enjoy because you'll be studying your subjects for two years.

A subject you studied at GCSE might be different at A-Level though, so do your research.

Do some research to find out if you might be interested in the subject.

Talk to the teachers at the sixth form about what the subject entails.

Which subjects do I enjoy at GCSE?

Do I want to try a new subject?

It's a good idea to pick subjects you think you'll be good at.

Ask current students what they like about the subject.

Check to see what the school or college recommends.

How many subjects should I take?

Make sure you'll have time to do all the work for the subjects you choose.

## ...But It's Also Important to Think Further Ahead

It might seem a <u>long way off</u>, but thinking about what you plan on doing <u>after your studies</u> can help you choose A-Levels that put you on the <u>right path</u>.

- Make sure you <u>choose A-Levels</u> that will help you <u>achieve your goals</u>. For example, if you want to study medicine at uni, you'll probably need to choose biology and chemistry A-Levels.

- Think about how your <u>combination</u> of A-Levels <u>work together</u> or <u>show off a range of skills</u> — whichever is more important for what you want to do.

- <u>Pick subjects</u> that you are <u>good at</u> or that you <u>enjoy</u> the most.

- Don't be afraid to try a <u>new subject</u>, but try to pick at least one <u>'core' subject</u> to keep your options open.

I know what I want to do after sixth form

I've got some ideas but I don't know for sure

I don't know what I want to do in the future

- Try to <u>pick subjects</u> that <u>fit your interests</u>.

- Look into a range of <u>higher-education courses</u>, <u>apprenticeships</u> or <u>jobs</u> that interest you, and see what A-Levels would help with them. Try to choose at least one <u>'core' subject</u> that could be relevant to them.

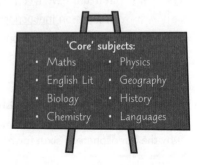

'Core' subjects:
- Maths
- English Lit
- Biology
- Chemistry
- Physics
- Geography
- History
- Languages

# Choosing Your A-Levels

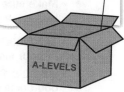

## Here are Some General Dos and Don'ts

### DO...

- <u>Research</u> each option properly. Find out <u>what the A-Level covers</u>, how it's <u>taught</u> and how it's <u>assessed</u>.

- Go to <u>taster sessions</u> if the school or college you're interested in offers them.

- <u>Talk</u> to current <u>A-Level students</u> and <u>teachers</u> about the subjects you're interested in. They can give you <u>advice</u> and answer your <u>questions</u>.

- Have a look at a range of schools and colleges, even if the one you took your <u>GCSEs</u> at has an <u>attached sixth form</u>. Different schools and colleges offer <u>different subjects</u> as well as a different overall <u>experience</u>.

### DON'T...

- Take a subject just because you think it's <u>expected of you</u>. A-Levels require a lot of <u>commitment</u>, so it needs to be something you <u>enjoy</u>.

- Pick a new subject <u>without doing any research</u>. You might not like the new subject.

- Assume you can <u>change your options</u> once you start Year 12. Lots of schools and colleges <u>do</u> allow you to make <u>some changes</u> early on in Year 12, but this can depend on your <u>timetable</u>.

- Take a subject just because your <u>friend</u> is doing it — you might have different <u>interests</u> and <u>abilities</u>.

## Think About Extra or Alternative Qualifications too

As A-Levels are just one of many options for post-16 study, you can also think about:

1) <u>BTECs</u> — BTECs are <u>vocational qualifications</u>. This means they have a more <u>work-related</u> focus and are usually <u>assessed</u> by completing <u>assignments during the course</u> rather than exams at the end. You can take BTECs in subjects like <u>business</u>, <u>engineering</u> and <u>ICT</u>. It's possible to take a <u>mixture</u> of A-Levels and BTECs if your school or college offers both. If you want to go to <u>university</u>, it's worth checking whether the universities you're interested in <u>accept BTECs</u>.

2) <u>The International Baccalaureate (IB)</u> — The IB is an <u>international qualification</u> that's taught in certain schools as an <u>alternative</u> to A-Levels. Students study a <u>broader range</u> of subjects through the IB. Like A-Levels, the IB course takes <u>two years</u> and is quite heavily <u>exam-based</u> (most subjects also include some element of <u>coursework</u> too).

3) <u>Extended Project Qualification (EPQ)</u> — The EPQ is an <u>extra qualification</u> that's often taken <u>alongside</u> A-Levels. It involves carrying out <u>research</u>, then completing a <u>5000-word essay</u>, a <u>production</u> or an <u>artefact</u> (see p.64-65). An EPQ is worth about half an A-Level and is popular with lots of <u>universities</u>.

---

### Eeny, meeny, miny, mo is definitely not the way to go...

Choosing your A-Levels can be really tough, but try not to get too overwhelmed by the number of options. Instead, see it as an opportunity to focus in on what you're interested in and to get excited about the future.

# Getting Organised

There isn't an 'i' in 'team', but there <u>is</u> one in 'organised', and during A-Levels it's especially important that you take responsibility for staying on top of your work. Luckily for you, these next pages are here to help.

## It's Important to Get Organised Early

Doing the following will give you the <u>best chance</u> of making sure you <u>don't get behind</u> on your work:

### Get into good habits

- Get a <u>good sleep pattern</u> in place (see p.37).
- Set up a <u>study space</u> at home. It's important to have somewhere you can get into <u>the right headspace</u> to focus on work (see p.11).

### Keep on top of any work

- Try not to leave your work until <u>the last minute</u>. You might find you end up with <u>too much</u> to do in a <u>short space of time</u> and can't finish everything. If you leave yourself more time, you're likely to produce <u>better quality work</u> and cause yourself <u>less stress</u> (see p.36-37).
- Get any work you've been asked to do in <u>on time</u>. If you start falling behind, you'll have to work <u>even harder</u> to <u>catch up</u>, so it's important to try to <u>keep on top of your work</u>.

### Go into each lesson prepared

- Make sure you have all the <u>equipment</u> you need for <u>each lesson</u>. Bringing some <u>spare stationery</u> is also a good idea.
- <u>Take notes</u> during class and then write them up neatly as part of your independent study (see p.14-15). It's also helpful to <u>file your notes</u> away <u>neatly</u> so you know where to find them when you come to <u>revise</u> or need to <u>look over a topic</u> (see below).

Mittens was suspicious of anything that involved the word 'early'.

## Learn How to Organise Your Notes Effectively

1) To keep organised, you'll need to <u>file things away</u> properly. This includes <u>notes</u>, <u>essays</u>, <u>class work</u>, <u>practice papers</u> and anything else that could come in useful for revision later.

2) If you plan to use folders, you'll probably want a <u>separate folder</u> for <u>each subject</u>. It's a good idea to use <u>ring binders</u> or <u>lever arch files</u> as they are sturdy and can hold lots of paper.

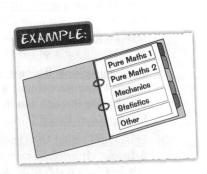

EXAMPLE:

Pure Maths 1
Pure Maths 2
Mechanics
Statistics
Other

3) Use <u>dividers</u> to separate the <u>different topics</u> in each subject folder. This will be useful if you're studying <u>different topics</u> at <u>the same time</u> and will make it easier to find certain information later on.

4) If you find you have <u>too many</u> hefty folders to carry around, try leaving your <u>big folders at home</u> and bringing <u>one folder to school</u> with the <u>most recent work</u> for all your subjects. If you do this, make sure you don't leave anything you might need behind.

5) Before starting Year 13, you'll probably need a <u>new set</u> of folders. <u>Keep hold</u> of your Year 12 ones, though. Having an <u>organised set of notes</u> will be incredibly important when you start <u>revising</u> towards the end of Year 13.

# Getting Organised

## Make Sure You Have the Right Resources

It's <u>difficult to stay organised</u> if you <u>don't have</u> the right <u>equipment</u> or access to the right <u>resources</u>.

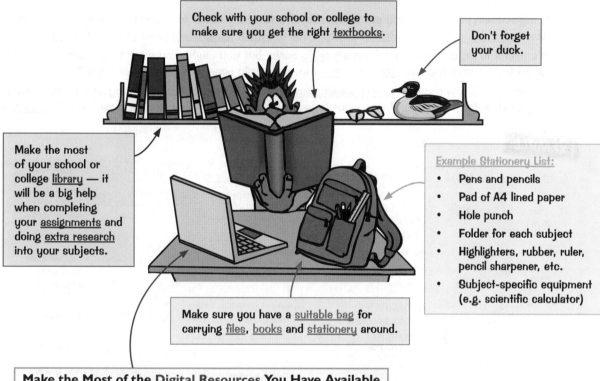

Check with your school or college to make sure you get the right <u>textbooks</u>.

Don't forget your duck.

Make the most of your school or college <u>library</u> — it will be a big help when completing your <u>assignments</u> and doing <u>extra research</u> into your subjects.

Example Stationery List:
- Pens and pencils
- Pad of A4 lined paper
- Hole punch
- Folder for each subject
- Highlighters, rubber, ruler, pencil sharpener, etc.
- Subject-specific equipment (e.g. scientific calculator)

Make sure you have a <u>suitable bag</u> for carrying <u>files</u>, <u>books</u> and <u>stationery</u> around.

## Make the Most of the Digital Resources You Have Available

- If you have a <u>computer</u> or <u>laptop</u> at home, make sure you have the <u>software</u> you need — <u>word processing software</u> will be useful for pretty much every subject.
- If you have a <u>printer</u> at home, make sure you <u>know how to use it</u> (you don't want to get stuck when the ink needs changing the night before your essay is due in).
- If you don't have a computer or printer at home, make sure you <u>get familiar</u> with how the <u>ones at school or college</u> work as early as possible.
- Make the most of your school or college's access to <u>online journals</u> or other <u>online resources</u> (see p.22).
- Consider using technology to help you <u>keep track</u> of the <u>tasks</u> you need to do (see p.9) and to help keep you <u>focused</u> when you study or revise (see p.25).

Keep your digital files organised:
- Make a folder for each subject and subfolders for each topic.
- Save things in a sensible place.
- Back up your files regularly.

## I take my duck everywhere — he helps me to quack on with my work...

You don't necessarily need to have a big lever arch file for each subject if you have another system that works. E.g. it might suit you better to use separate notepads, or you might prefer typing all your notes up on a computer.

# Getting Organised

This next bit's all about calendars, diaries and to-do lists. It might not sound like the stuff that dreams are made of, but if your dream is to pass your A-Levels, the next two pages are definitely worth a read.

## It's Really Important to Plan Your Time

1) It might seem like you've only got a few subjects to worry about at A-Level, but it's important to use a <u>calendar</u>, <u>diary</u> or <u>timetable</u> to keep track of <u>dates</u>, <u>assignments</u> and (eventually) <u>revision</u>.

2) It's useful to organise your work on a <u>weekly</u> basis, but you might also want to consider organising your study across a whole <u>month</u> or <u>term</u> too, especially nearer to exams (see page 71).

3) The example below shows a <u>typical weekly timetable</u> for a Year 13 student studying History, French and English Literature. You might also want to include a column for what you have planned <u>after school</u>.

EXAMPLE:

| Date | 9.15-10.15 | 10.15-11.15 | Break | 11.30-12.30 | Lunch | 13.30-14.30 | 14.30-16.00 |
|---|---|---|---|---|---|---|---|
| Mon 02/11 | French • Essay due ☆ | History • Tudors lesson • Research assignment due ☆ | | Free Period • Work on French exercises | | Free period • Start research for History essay | English Literature • Poetry lesson • Commentary due ☆ |
| Tue 03/11 | Free period • Work on uni application | Free period • Work on EPQ | | English Literature • Poetry lesson | | French • Grammar lesson | History • Cold War lesson • Essay writing workshop |
| Wed 04/11 | French • Grammar exercises due ☆ | Free period • Start history essay and complete extra research | | History • Tudors lesson | Piano lesson | Free period • Work on EPQ | Sport • Basketball |
| Thu 05/11 | Tutor Group • Work on personal statements | Free period • Rehearse English Lit presentation | | English Literature • Jane Eyre lesson • Presentation to the class ☆ | | Free period • Work on uni application | French • Film screening |
| Fri 06/11 | History • Cold War Lesson • Essay due ☆ | English Literature • Jane Eyre lesson | | Free period • Organise notes | Debating club | Free period • Work on English essay | Enrichment • Community involvement |

## Don't Forget About the Weekend

1) It's important to take some time to <u>relax</u> at the weekend, but it's also a good opportunity to <u>catch up</u> on your work and get any <u>tasks</u> that need doing for next week <u>out of the way</u>.

2) It's a good idea to <u>organise</u> your weekend tasks. You might find it helpful to include rows for Saturday and Sunday in your <u>weekly calendar</u>, or you could make a <u>separate weekend plan</u>.

Billy liked to use the weekend to chill with his mates.

# Getting Organised

## Use To-Do Lists to Keep on Top of Your Work

1) As well as having a diary or calendar, it's a good idea to keep a to-do list of all the tasks you need to finish each week.

2) Try to keep this neat and tidy, so it's clear what you have to do and when you have to do it by. Make sure you leave yourself room to add more tasks as the week goes on.

3) The example on the right matches the timetable on the previous page. It gives you an idea of how to use a weekly timetable and a to-do list together to keep track of your tasks. You could break some of these tasks down into smaller chunks if you wanted (see next page).

4) Try to get into the habit of adding a task to your to-do list as soon as you've been given it. This will make sure you don't forget to do anything.

**EXAMPLE:**

| Task | Due Date | Done? |
|---|---|---|
| Complete French essay | 02/11 | ✓ |
| Finish History research assignment | 02/11 | ✓ |
| Complete poetry commentary | 02/11 | ✓ |
| Read next set of poems from anthology | 03/11 | ✓ |
| Submit personal statement draft to tutor | 03/11 | |
| Complete French grammar exercises | 04/11 | |
| Prepare Jane Eyre presentation | 05/11 | |
| Finish Cold War essay | 06/11 | |

## There are Different Ways of Making a To-Do List

You don't have to make a traditional to-do list if you have a system that works better for you. Here are some alternatives you could try:

### Using sticky notes to keep track of tasks

- Write each task on a separate sticky note and throw it away when the task is done.
- You could colour code your sticky notes by using a different colour for each subject.
- Once you have a set of tasks, you can reprioritise your tasks by moving the sticky notes around.

**X**

Using a calendar app:

- You can set reminders so that you receive a notification before an assignment is due.
- You can delete or hide tasks when you've done them, so it's clearer to see what you still have left to do.
- It's easy to edit your to-do list and calendar if your plans change.
- If your to-do list is on your phone, you can carry it around with you easily.

## Dear Diary, today I've got to finish writing page 13...

No, that's not the kind of diary that will come in useful... That said, don't be afraid to use your own methods if they work for you. Different people have different lives, so there's no 'one size fits all' way of staying organised.

# Motivating Yourself

Studying for A-Levels is tough, and it can be hard to stay motivated when you've got a pile of work taller than a giraffe in high-heeled shoes. That's where these tips for motivating yourself come in handy.

## ① Split your work up into manageable chunks

- Don't give yourself too much to do at once. Splitting your work up into smaller tasks will make it seem less daunting and help you feel more motivated to get on with it.

- Use a timetable and to-do list to plan your time and keep track of your workload (see previous pages). The act of ticking things off your to-do list will remind you of the progress you've made.

**Sociology Essay**
- Do some research
- Make a plan
- Write first draft
- Re-read and edit essay

Clara used food-based rewards to help her focus.

- Give yourself a reward for completing a task. For example, you could reward yourself by watching a TV show or going for a walk. If you have a to-do list, you can plan these rewards ahead of time so you have something to look forward to.

- Remember to take regular breaks. It's easier to motivate yourself and work efficiently if you split your time into chunks, rather than trying to do everything in one sitting. Even if you feel like you've not got much done, taking breaks is important.

## ② Maintain a study-life balance

- If you have a good study-life balance, you'll feel more motivated to work because you'll know that work isn't the only thing you're doing all day. At times, it might seem like you don't have time for anything except studying, but it's important to take time out from your work to do things you enjoy, such as playing a sport or learning a musical instrument. Otherwise, you might get study fatigue or burn yourself out before exam season.

- As well as being good for your mental health, hobbies and interests also show employers or universities that you're a well-rounded person.

**EXAMPLE:**

**Here's an example of how you could fit your hobbies into your evening plans:**

- 5.00-5.45 pm — Dinner (or tea if you're from the northern realms)
- 5.45-6.45 pm — Biology assignment
- 6.45-7.30 pm — Go on a walk with friends
- 7.30-8.00 pm — Read next batch of poems

If you know that you're planning to meet your friends at 6.45, you'll be more motivated to get your biology work finished.

By the time you start doing your English work, you'll feel refreshed and energised after taking a break to exercise.

# Motivating Yourself

③ ~~Don't get distracted by the giraffe~~ Find a productive study space

- It's hard to keep yourself motivated if you don't have a <u>good study space</u>. There are <u>different places</u> you can study — most people use <u>different ones</u> at <u>different times</u>:

See page 25 for advice on setting up your revision space.

### The Library

👍 It's quiet and is specifically designed to help you study.

👎 You can only use the school or college library when you're on site. Public libraries aren't always open and might involve travel time.

### Your Bedroom

👍 You can set up your study space as you want.

👎 It's easy to get distracted and lose motivation to work.

### Somewhere With a Friend

👍 You can discuss your work and motivate each other.

👎 There's a danger you could distract each other.

- Wherever you decide to study, try to <u>avoid distractions</u>. This means finding somewhere that's <u>calm</u> and <u>putting away your phone</u>. This will make it easier to <u>stay focused</u> by keeping you <u>engaged in your work</u>.

④ <u>Focus on your goals</u>

- One of the keys to staying motivated is to <u>remind yourself</u> of your <u>long-term goals</u>.

- This will help to keep you <u>focused</u> on <u>why you're studying</u> and <u>why it's important</u> that you continue to <u>work hard</u>. Your long-term goals could include:

  ✓ getting into a <u>good university</u> to study a course you're really interested in

  ✓ achieving the qualifications you need to one day get your <u>dream job</u>

  ✓ proving to yourself and others that you can be <u>successful</u>

- It can also be motivating to think about your <u>short-term goals</u>, e.g. to do well in your next <u>practice essay</u>.

- <u>Don't compare</u> yourself to other people — they'll have their <u>own set of goals</u>.

**It's easy to get distracted, so make sure you ooh look — I found a new colour!**

Procrastination can be a real problem, which is why it's important to avoid distractions and take regular breaks. If you find that you just can't get started on a piece of work, try beginning with a simpler task to ease yourself in.

# Different Learning Styles

Learning styles are like apples — they come in different varieties and go really well with cheese. No, wait — just the first bit. Anyway, knowing which styles of learning suit you is handy when it comes to studying.

## There are Four Main Learning Styles

1) There's no one 'right' way to learn or revise, but if you know which styles work best for you, it can help you to decide which study techniques will be most useful throughout your A-Levels.

2) Most people identify with one or two of these learning styles more than the others, but they often benefit from using a mixture of them — this also adds variety to the time spent studying.

- Some people prefer learning visually — they learn best by using diagrams and graphic representations.
- Useful learning techniques include making flash cards or mind maps, colour coding notes and illustrating material with pictures or diagrams.

- Some people work best aurally — they learn by speaking and listening.
- Helpful learning techniques include reading material out loud, listening to podcasts on course topics, making up mnemonics and discussing topics with friends.

- Some people learn best through reading and writing.
- Helpful learning techniques include taking notes and reading through them, making lists, doing extra reading, and sorting ideas using headings and bullet points.

- Some people prefer learning physically — they learn best by doing things, such as activities or experiments.
- Useful learning techniques include incorporating real-world examples into notes and finding ways to include physical activity when you study (e.g. taking a walk).

3) There's more about the different techniques you could use for study and revision on pages 28-31.

## I tried studying in a cupboard, but it really cramped my style...

Learning styles aren't an exact science, but having an idea about the ways you learn best will help you to organise your study time. It'll also help you study more effectively by focusing on the techniques that you find most useful.

# Different Coffee Styles

Another thing that comes in different styles is coffee, and your sixth form will likely have some form of café or canteen where you can grab a cup. If you don't know your latte from your mocha, this page is for you.

## CGP Coffee Shop

### Black Coffee
Pure and simple — ground coffee beans are placed in a filter and hot water is run through them.

### ~~Expresso~~ Espresso
Small but mighty — espresso is a concentrated form of black coffee that's made by forcing pressurised water through ground coffee beans.

*Espresso comes in 'shots' — a shot can be drunk by itself, but it can also form the base of many different coffee drinks.*

### Americano
A fancier black coffee — an americano has a similar look and taste to black coffee, but is made by adding hot water to a shot of espresso.

### Red Eye
Black coffeeee — a cup of black coffee with a shot of espresso added in for good measure.

### Sorry I'm Latte
Milky goodness — a latte consists of a shot of espresso topped up with steamed milk and a thin layer of foam.

### Cappuccino
A latte foam — like a latte, but with a thicker layer of foam and some chocolate powder on the top.

### Flat White
A latte less milk — like a latte but with more espresso and less steamed milk for a stronger taste.

*A latte, cappuccino and flat white are all quite similar — the main difference lies in the ratio of different elements.*

### Iced Coffee
The coolest option — coffee mixed with cubes of ice.

### Frappé
Cold coffee slushie — like an iced coffee, but the coffee is mixed with blended or crushed ice.

### Mocha Exam
Coffee / chocolate combo — a shot of espresso combined with chocolate powder and steamed milk, topped with foam.

### Affogato Do My Homework
Ice cream goodness — yep, an affogato involves a shot (or two) of espresso and a great big dollop of ice cream.

## Now we've bean through all that, let's move on to the next page like a shot...

Okay, so your sixth form might not have all these, but what's to stop you making a homemade affogato to kick off your independent study? I wouldn't recommend carrying a tub of ice cream around in your bag all day though...

# Independent Study

One of the biggest differences between GCSE and A-Level is the level of independent study that's involved. To be successful at A-Level, it's important to spend time studying during your free periods and after school.

## Independent Study is Crucial at A-Level

1) <u>Engaging</u> with your subjects outside of class helps to <u>improve your understanding</u> of them.

2) By taking more <u>responsibility</u> for your own work, you'll <u>develop important skills</u>, such as <u>critical thinking</u>, <u>time management</u> and <u>self-discipline</u>. These are valued by <u>universities</u> and <u>employers</u>, as they're vital for success in higher education and in many jobs.

Gerry and Terry spent plenty of time studying the inside of their eyelids.

## There are Various Ways of Studying Independently

Independent study doesn't have to mean sitting alone with a book — try these ideas:

### Go over content from class

- <u>Read through</u> the notes you've made and <u>write them up neatly</u> to <u>consolidate</u> what you've learnt (see pages 16-17).

- Spend <u>extra time</u> on <u>topics</u> you found <u>difficult</u> to <u>make sure you understand</u> them.

### Study with your friends

- <u>Read through notes</u> together or <u>try testing each other</u> on material you've learnt, e.g. definitions or formulas.

- <u>Practise presentations</u> with an audience to <u>gain confidence</u>, or hold <u>mock debates</u> on topics you've studied in class to help you <u>develop ideas and arguments</u>.

### Prepare for future classes

- Complete any <u>work</u> you've been set, read any <u>set texts</u> for upcoming topics and <u>study for any tests</u> you have.

### Find activities related to your subjects

- Choose <u>areas</u> of your subjects that <u>interest</u> you and look for ways that you can <u>engage</u> with them.

- See if there are any <u>groups</u> that you could <u>join</u>, e.g. an <u>astronomy group</u> to help <u>improve your physics knowledge</u>.

- Find things you could <u>watch</u> or <u>listen</u> to that are <u>useful</u> for your subjects, e.g. watching foreign films will <u>increase your exposure</u> to another language.

## You Can Do Other Things with Your Independent Study Time

- Work towards an <u>extra qualification</u> such as an <u>EPQ</u> (see pages 64-65) or another <u>certificate</u> or <u>award</u> that's related to your subjects or interests.

- Depending on what stage you're at, you could begin <u>researching future options</u> or <u>working on applications</u>, e.g. for university, an apprenticeship or a job.

# Independent Study

## Work Out How Much Time to Spend Per Subject

For more on studying your specific subjects, see p.38-65.

1) The <u>amount of time</u> you should spend studying outside of class will depend on <u>what subjects</u> you're studying.

2) Some subjects may require more independent study time than others — e.g. you might want to <u>spend more time</u> on subjects with <u>lots of reading</u> (e.g. English Literature) or <u>practical work</u> (e.g. Fine Art).

3) The amount of time you spend is <u>your choice</u> — don't feel like you have to do the same amount as a friend. However, <u>any extra study</u> you can do during your A-Levels will help you to <u>understand</u> your subjects <u>better</u> — this will make it <u>easier</u> when you come <u>to revise</u>.

4) It's important to <u>plan your independent study time</u> so that you can make the most of it. Make sure you know <u>what</u> you're going to do <u>when</u>, and try to <u>spread out your subjects</u> and other commitments throughout the week to add <u>variety</u> (see pages 8-9).

Lia wasn't taking any chances when it came to working out her independent study time.

## Make the Most of Your Free Periods

1) You're likely to have <u>free periods</u> during your A-Levels. It might be tempting to spend the time chatting with your friends, but using them <u>productively</u> will give you more time for the things you enjoy <u>outside of school</u>.

2) Make the most of the <u>spare time</u> and the <u>resources</u> in your school or college to do some <u>independent study</u>.

## Change How and Where You're Going to Study

Vary your <u>methods</u> and find <u>different places</u> where you can study independently — a <u>change of scenery</u> can help to keep things feeling fresh and less repetitive. You could try:

- Writing up notes in the <u>library</u> or <u>common room</u> in your free periods
- Going to a <u>café with your friends</u> to discuss topics from class
- Watching a documentary <u>at home</u> with your family or friends
- Listening to a podcast related to your subject while you <u>go for a walk</u>

I'm free!

**In America, a free period looks something like this** ⟶ .

Learning to study independently can be a challenge, but it's a great skill to learn for later life and it'll definitely help you succeed at A-Level. Take time to plan your own study and include plenty of variety in your schedule.

# How to Make Effective Notes

Whether you're writing them for the first time or using them to revise, notes are something you'll need to use almost every day of your A-Levels, so it's important to know how to make them as useful as possible.

## Effective Note-Taking is an Active Process

1) You should take notes when you're in class (e.g. when your teacher is explaining a new concept) as well as when you're doing extra research (e.g. when you're reading for an essay).

2) Taking notes is about more than just copying things down — it involves engaging with what you're reading or listening to and then recording the key information in your own words. Thinking about things more actively makes it easier to understand and remember the information later on.

Catticus was always there to lend a helping paw when Meera was taking notes.

## Make Sure You Take Effective Notes in Class...

1) The notes that you take in class don't need to be perfect.

2) It's more important to listen to your teacher and make sure you understand the topic or concept they're talking about than it is to scribble down everything they're saying.

3) Focus on writing down the key points in your own words — you can revisit these later on and add in more information.

4) Mark up your notes to highlight anything that your teacher puts special emphasis on, e.g. you could put an asterisk beside anything that is especially important for the exam.

**EXAMPLE:**

Here's an example of how you might write some psychology notes in class.

Attachment — close bond between infant and caregiver

Common features of caregiver-infant interactions:

- Sensitive responsiveness — responding to the infant
- Imitation — infant copies actions. Meltzoff and Moore (1977)
- Interactional synchrony — infant reacts in time with speech. Condon and Sander (1974)
- Reciprocity / turn-taking
- Motherese — high-pitched way of talking to infants

## ...Then Neaten Up and Organise Your Notes Later

1) After class, go back over your notes and create a new, neat and easy-to-follow version that fleshes out the key points — this will reinforce the content for you and make the notes easier to use later on.

2) Make sure that your notes include all the information you need to know. You can do this by looking in textbooks or using online resources (see page 26 for more).

3) Use a mixture of techniques to draw attention to key info, but be selective with what you focus on:
   - Add subheadings to your notes to organise the information.
   - Use highlighting to pick out the most important points.
   - Colour-code information to show links, e.g. write definitions in orange or formulas in blue.

# How to Make Effective Notes

 **EXAMPLE:**

This example shows how you could write up the psychology notes from the previous page to make them more useful.

*It's a good idea to keep a back-up copy of your notes — you could take photos of handwritten notes or put typed-up notes on a USB drive.*

<u>Attachment</u> — the close emotional bond between an infant and caregiver

<u>Common Features of Caregiver-Infant Interactions</u>

These help to form and maintain attachment:

1. <u>Sensitive responsiveness</u> — Caregiver reacts appropriately to signals from infant, e.g. offering comfort when the infant shows signs of distress.

2. <u>Imitation</u> — Infant copies caregiver's actions and behaviour. <u>Meltzoff and Moore (1977)</u> found infants aged 2-3 weeks seemed to imitate facial expressions and hand movements.

3. <u>Interactional synchrony</u> — Infants move and react to the rhythm of the caregiver's speech (called a 'conversation dance'). <u>Condon and Sander (1974)</u> showed that infants seem to move in time with adult's conversations.

4. <u>Reciprocity / turn-taking</u> — Caregivers and infants respond to each other and take it in turns to act.

5. <u>Motherese</u> — Slow, high-pitched speech used with infant. No evidence this has an impact on the strength of the attachment between a caregiver and infant.

## Try Different Methods of Note-Taking

The example above is just <u>one way</u> you could put your notes together — feel free to <u>experiment</u> and find the way that's <u>most effective</u> for you. Here are a few other <u>popular methods</u>:

- <u>Outlining method</u> — use levels of indented numbers, letters and bullets to organise your notes into <u>main points</u>, <u>sub points</u>, and <u>extra info</u>.
- <u>Cornell method</u> — have a small column for <u>key words</u> and a larger column for your <u>main notes</u>, then add a <u>summary</u> at the bottom.
- <u>Writing on handouts</u> — if you're given a <u>copy</u> of a presentation or some printed notes by your teacher, you could add your notes to these. This can be a good way to <u>expand</u> on the ideas and concepts you've discussed <u>without</u> having to take <u>extensive notes</u>.

*Jasmine's mum wasn't convinced by her claim that she had an organised note-taking method.*

## I made some notes on map reading, but I seem to have lost them...

Making sure that you're comfortable taking notes early on in your A-Levels will be really beneficial — not only will they help you learn, but spending time on them throughout your course will make revision easier too (see p.26).

# Essay Writing

Even if you've written essays for a piece of classwork, coursework or non-exam assessment before, it's worth looking over these pages — they're full of advice for making the process easier.  Let's begin...

## Make Sure You Understand the Question

1) Highlight any key words in the question and make sure you fully understand what you're being asked to do.

2) It can be easy to go off in a different direction once you've started writing, but keeping these key words in mind will help you stay focused on answering the question.

Maja learnt lots of key words — lock, master, skeleton, car, house...

## Jot Down Your Initial Thoughts

1) When you first read the question, write down your initial ideas about what you might cover and what (if any) research you need to carry out.

2) Think about whether you could make your essay more original — e.g. if there are ways you could approach the question from an unusual angle or include sources that aren't on your reading list.

3) At this stage, it's also important to decide how you'll use your time.  Make sure you leave yourself enough time to research, write and proofread your essay before the deadline.

## Do Some Research To Develop Your Thoughts

You might need to include some research in your essay to support your arguments and to show that you've explored the topic more widely.

- Use your notes from class, your independent study notes and your initial ideas to guide your research.

- Look for a range of sources that you could discuss in your essay and make careful notes on any research that you do (see pages 22-23).

- Think about whether the research changes your perspective on the question — this will help you to shape your ideas before you write a proper plan.

Keep track of which sources you use — this will make it easier when you come to reference things and compile a bibliography (see page 23).

# Essay Writing

## Make a Plan for Your Essay

1) Use everything you've done so far to help you choose the main points you want to cover in your essay.

2) The amount of detail in an essay plan can vary, but you need to make sure it has a clear structure — this will help you to cover your main points without repeating yourself or going off track.

3) Most essays have an introduction, a series of paragraphs that follow a logical order, and a conclusion. There's more about how to write each of these on the next page, but keep this overall structure in mind when planning.

4) Once you've ordered your points, go back over your plan to check that it covers everything you need to answer the question — if you're being tested on certain assessment objectives (AOs), make sure your plan covers them all.

**EXAMPLE:**

Here's an example plan for a sociology essay.

'Evaluate the idea that factors inside school are the key reason for the differences in educational achievement between genders in the UK.'

Para 1 — **Introduction**. In the UK, girls outperform boys at all stages of education — e.g. better GCSE and A-Level results & more girls at university. Outline main reasons — some relate to factors in schools, but others to external factors.

Para 2 — **In-school — school labelling**. Jackson (1998) — negative labelling of boys by schools. Lower expectations can lead to self-fulfilling prophecy for grades and behaviour.

Para 3 — **In-school — interactions with teachers**. Swann and Graddol (1993) — girls have better-quality interactions with teachers than boys do. Mitsos and Browne (1998) suggest the feminisation of teaching gives girls more positive role models.

Para 4 — **In-school — educational policy**. Introduction of National Curriculum (1988) and other government initiatives gave girls more encouragement in traditionally 'male' subjects (e.g. STEM subjects), leading to an increase in achievement.

Para 5 — **External — anti-discrimination policy**. The Equal Pay Act (1971) and the Sex Discrimination Act (1975) helped to create more equal opportunities and changed values in society. This has changed attitudes in schools about what girls can achieve.

Para 6 — **External — social expectations.** Sharpe (1994) — change in expectations affecting educational achievement. The impact of the changing labour market and family structures means girls and their families have different expectations about their futures.

Para 7 — **Conclusion**. Internal factors play an important role in educational achievement but are a reflection of external factors in society which have a bigger impact — changes in societal values have affected attitudes, expectations and policy about girls' achievement in schools.

# Essay Writing

When you've finished researching and planning, it's time to get to the really exciting bit — writing the essay.

## Write the First Draft of Your Essay

It can be daunting to stare at a blank page, but when you start writing, remember that this is a <u>first draft</u> — it doesn't have to be perfect.  Start by drafting your <u>introduction</u>, then go on to the <u>rest of the essay</u>:

**INTRO**
- This is where you'll make it <u>clear</u> how you're going to <u>approach</u> the question.
- Include a <u>rough outline</u> of the <u>points</u> you're going to discuss during your essay — use some of the <u>question wording</u> so it's easy to see that you're <u>focused</u> on the task.
- <u>Return</u> to your introduction after writing your essay to make any <u>necessary changes</u>.

**MAIN BODY**
- You need to write a <u>paragraph</u> for each of the <u>points</u> in your plan.
- <u>Support</u> all of your points with <u>evidence</u>, then <u>explain</u> and <u>develop</u> them.
- <u>Engage critically</u> with sources — use your research material as a springboard for your <u>essay discussion</u> and show how your research <u>supports</u> your points.
- <u>Linking</u> your points back to the question wording will keep your essay <u>focused</u> and <u>demonstrate</u> that you're answering the question.

**CONCLUSION**
- This is where you'll <u>summarise</u> your main points.
- Try to finish with a sentence or remark that <u>wraps everything up nicely</u> — end your essay <u>positively</u> by showing how you've <u>successfully answered the question</u>.

*Follow your plan closely when you're writing to make sure that you cover all of your points.*

## Leave Time to Edit Your Essay

1) Once you've finished your first draft, try to give yourself a bit of time away from your essay — some <u>distance</u> will help you return to it with fresh eyes.

2) When you come back to it, <u>read over</u> what you've written — check that you've worded your points <u>clearly</u>, that they <u>flow</u> smoothly, and that you haven't gone over the <u>word count</u>.

3) If you have time, you could <u>ask someone</u> you trust (e.g. a parent or a sibling) to read over your essay.  <u>Think carefully</u> about their suggestions and then <u>edit</u> your essay <u>as needed</u>.

4) Remember to <u>proofread</u> the final draft of your essay before you submit it — use this time to <u>check for small mistakes</u> rather than trying to change the whole structure.

Dahyun liked to get as much distance as possible from her essay before she started editing it.

*Be prepared to write multiple drafts of your essay — this will help you develop your ideas and polish what you've written.*

# Essay Writing

## Use This Essay Writing Checklist

Keep referring to this checklist <u>while writing</u> your essay, then tick everything off <u>at the end</u>:

- ☑ Have I answered the question fully?
- ☑ Have I used a clear structure?
- ☑ Have I supported my points with well-researched evidence?
- ☑ Have I cited research correctly?
- ☑ Have I met any word count limits?
- ☑ Have I used correct spelling, punctuation and grammar throughout?

*The way you write essays can vary across subjects, so you might want to adapt this checklist for your subjects.*

## Writing Essays in Exams is Slightly Different

If you have to write an <u>essay</u> or answer an <u>extended-response question</u> in an exam, you won't be able to spend nearly <u>as much time</u> on your answer, but you should still try to do the following:

1) Highlight the <u>key words</u> when you first read the question so that you can <u>focus</u> on them while planning and writing.

2) <u>Plan</u> your answer — you won't be able to do this in as much depth, but it's important to jot down a <u>rough structure</u> before you start writing.

3) Include <u>evidence</u> to support your points. For example, you'll need to include quotes for English Literature and relevant research for Sociology or Psychology. Include any <u>extra information</u> — e.g. for a study, you should include the <u>name</u> of the researcher and (if needed) the <u>year</u> it was published.

4) If you're <u>struggling to remember</u> a specific quote, name, date or research finding in the exam, just write about it <u>more generally</u> — this will be better than panicking and <u>wasting time</u>.

5) <u>Leave some time</u> at the end of the exam to <u>read through</u> your essay. <u>Check</u> you've answered the question and <u>make changes</u> if you need to.

It was going to take Cameron forever to write the essay under these exam conditions.

*Make sure you get some timed practice writing exam essays both during your course and as part of your revision (see pages 34-35).*

## Research, plan, write, proofread — need essay more?

The key to a great essay is planning properly, using your plan to write a tightly structured essay that answers the question, and leaving time to check your work so you can make sure your essay is at its best when you submit it.

# How to Do Research

You probably won't have had to do much academic research before now, but knowing how to find and use different sources is a key part of success at A-Level. These pages are packed with useful tips to help you.

## There are Lots of Places to Find Information

1) There are <u>plenty of places</u> you can <u>find sources</u> when you begin researching:

### Resources at your school or college

- <u>Ask your teachers</u> for <u>extra reading recommendations</u> that you can use to begin your research.

- Go to your school or college <u>library</u> — they'll probably have <u>books related to your subject</u> as well as <u>magazine or journal subscriptions</u> you can use.

### Online databases

- The <u>internet</u> is a great place to find <u>journal articles</u> or <u>news reports</u> related to your subject — search for <u>keywords</u> and <u>topics</u> to see what you can find.

- <u>Google Scholar</u>™, <u>JSTOR</u>®, and <u>DOAJ</u> (the Directory of Open Access Journals) are online databases with plenty of academic material you can use for research.

- Some journals might be behind a <u>paywall</u>, so find out whether your <u>school or college</u> has an online <u>subscription</u>.

### References from your research

- If you find a <u>book</u> or <u>article</u> that's useful for your research, try looking at the <u>academic works cited</u> in it for further information — sources will usually include a <u>bibliography</u> (a list of all the works that have been used).

- If you <u>watch</u> or <u>listen</u> to something related to your subject, see whether there's any <u>programme information online</u> with <u>recommended resources</u> or details of <u>experts</u> who were involved — these can help you find out more about the topic.

2) If you find a <u>book</u> that looks like it might have potential, check the <u>contents</u> or <u>index</u> for <u>relevant sections</u> — this is a <u>quick way</u> of judging whether it's worth looking through the rest of the book. <u>Introductions</u>, <u>forewords</u> and <u>abstracts</u> can also be useful for some subjects, e.g. English Literature.

## Engage Critically with Your Research

1) When you first read or watch something, focus on understanding its <u>main arguments</u> or <u>ideas</u> so you can <u>think critically</u> about it.

2) The next time you read or watch it, <u>take notes</u> so that you have a <u>record</u> of its <u>key points</u> and any particularly useful <u>ideas</u> or <u>quotes</u>. You could do this on a <u>separate piece of paper</u> or <u>annotate the material</u> if you have your own copy.

3) <u>Don't ignore</u> sources that present <u>arguments or theories</u> that <u>differ</u> to <u>your own view</u> — it's important to <u>read</u> and <u>engage</u> with these critically so that you can <u>broaden your ideas</u> and create a <u>balanced argument</u>.

Laura had so much fun doing her history research that she forgot all about her essay.

# How to Do Research

## Consider the Credibility of Your Sources

1) When looking at a source, it's important to think about how credible it is. You should think about:

- Type of source — some sources, such as academic books and articles, are likely to be more thoroughly researched and credible than something like a blog post.
- Author expertise — if the type of source isn't that credible, find out if the author has any qualifications or experience in the field.
- Bias — check whether the author only includes one side of the argument — if they do, think about why this might be.

2) Every source you use should be credible, but you should also think about any limitations they have. For example, think about when the source was published and whether its contents are still relevant to the subject today — the findings might have been superseded by newer research.

3) Comment on these limitations and explore the implications of them in your analysis, e.g. "While Merlin's study on the dangers of wild dragons makes an important contribution to the field, it was written in 1965, so doesn't take into account more recent efforts to..."

## Keep a Record of Any Research You Do

1) You'll need to cite any sources that you use in your work. Check with your teachers to see if there's a specific referencing system you should use.

2) You should at least include the author and date of anything you reference, e.g. "They concluded that 'crocodiles do not make great pets' (CGP 2020)".

3) You might have to put together a bibliography — keep track of the key information you'll need for this so you can compile one easily. You could even try using reference management software to help.

4) It's vital that you don't plagiarise anybody else's work — even if you haven't quoted something directly, you need to acknowledge where the ideas or evidence came from and reference them properly.

5) Once you've finished your essay, file away your research notes and source list in case you need to refer to them later.

Things to Keep Note of:

- Author(s) of the work
- Date of the work
- Title of the book or article, and (if needed) the chapter
- Book edition / journal volume and issue number
- Page reference of the material

---

## Ketchup, salad cream, barbecue, cranberry — all credible sauces...

The more research you do, the easier it'll be to find and engage with useful sources. Don't forget to evaluate the credibility of everything you research and make sure you provide references for all the sources you've used.

# Getting Started

It's time to address the elephant in the book — revision. Yes, this section covers everything from music and mind maps to mark schemes and memory techniques. First up is a couple of pages on starting your revision.

## Don't Start Revising Too Early

1) While it's important to <u>keep your exams in mind</u> throughout your <u>A-Levels</u>, you <u>can't start revising properly</u> until you know all the <u>course content</u>, so focus on <u>learning</u> and <u>understanding</u> it before you start revising.

2) If you enter revision mode <u>too soon</u>, there's also the risk that you'll <u>burn out</u> or have <u>forgotten information</u> by the time the exams come around.

3) You should still <u>go back over your notes</u> throughout the course, though — it's a good idea to do this <u>routinely</u> in your <u>independent study time</u> (see pages 14-15). This should help to <u>refresh your knowledge</u> and help you <u>make links</u> between topics.

4) Most people shift their focus to <u>exam revision</u> about <u>two months</u> before their first exam — this amount of time will <u>vary</u> for different people, depending on how they work best.

5) Try to avoid starting <u>so late</u> that you <u>run out of time</u> to revise everything properly. However, even if you start later than you'd like, there are still lots of <u>things you can do</u> to prepare for the exams.

David hoped that by pretending it was the 1700s, he'd still have time to revise for his exams.

## Make a Plan That Covers Everything You Have to Revise

Working out <u>what content</u> you have to revise will help you to plan <u>how much time</u> you need. This will also help you break your revision up into <u>manageable chunks</u>, so it seems like less of a <u>mammoth task</u>.

- Decide <u>how confident</u> you feel about each topic using a <u>topic planner</u> (see page 70) — this will help you work out <u>which topics</u> you need to <u>dedicate more time to</u>.

- Use a <u>revision timetable</u> (see pages 70-73) to <u>plan out your revision</u> — this will help you make sure that you've got <u>enough time</u> to <u>focus on each subject</u> before the exams.

- Start thinking <u>early on</u> about <u>what kind of revision</u> might work best for you. The methods you use might depend on your <u>subject</u> — e.g. for <u>maths</u> you might focus on <u>exam practice</u> as soon as possible, and for <u>biology</u> you might focus on using <u>mind maps</u> and <u>flash cards</u> to <u>consolidate your knowledge</u> before applying it to exam questions.

# Getting Started

Ignore me — I'm irrelephant...

## Make Sure You Have a Productive Revision Space

Having a good <u>place to revise</u> is just as important as having a good <u>place to study</u> (see p.11). Here are some tips on how to set yourself up for <u>productive revision</u>:

### Make sure you're comfortable

- <u>Tidy</u> your study space before your first revision session. This can make the space feel <u>fresh again</u> and help to get you in the <u>revision mindset</u>.

- Try to work in a <u>well-lit</u> room so it's easy to read. Make sure you have all the <u>stationery</u> you need nearby, and do your best to avoid any <u>potential distractions</u>.

- Make sure you've got a <u>proper seat</u> (e.g. a desk chair) and you're <u>comfortable</u> sitting in it for a <u>long time</u>. <u>Don't</u> be tempted to revise <u>in bed</u> — the urge to nap can sometimes be a bit too <u>overwhelming</u>...

### Set the volume

- It's generally a good idea to find a revision space that's <u>quiet</u> so you can <u>concentrate</u>.

- However, some people prefer working with a bit of <u>background noise</u>. Listening to <u>instrumental music</u> can be good if it helps you to <u>relax</u> and stay <u>focused</u>.

- Listening to <u>podcasts</u> or <u>audio books</u> while you're doing another revision task is likely to be a bit <u>too distracting</u>, though.

Even if you've set up your <u>perfect revision space</u>, it can be helpful to try working <u>somewhere else</u> if you're <u>lacking motivation</u>. Sometimes, working in a space where <u>others are working</u> can help you to <u>focus</u>.

## Gather All the Tools You Need to Help You Revise

1) Make sure you have <u>everything you need</u> for revision <u>nearby</u>, e.g. notes, textbooks, stationery, snacks and drink.

2) You might also want to set up any <u>technology</u> you're going to use to help you <u>maintain your focus</u>. For example, you could:

- Use a <u>timer</u> to <u>keep track</u> of each revision session — this will <u>motivate you</u> to keep working until your <u>next break</u>.

- Try downloading a <u>study app</u> — there are apps that <u>remind you when to take breaks</u>, and others that help you stay focused by <u>limiting the amount of time</u> you can spend on <u>social media</u> and other <u>distractions</u>.

Anne recognised the importance of having snacks nearby at all times.

## I revise at the bowling alley after hours — it's so quiet, you can hear a pin drop...

It's not always true that the longer you revise, the more you'll learn. You're likely to take in more content from doing two hours of focused revision than you will from flicking through your notes distractedly for four hours.

# Compiling Your Notes

Remember those neat, helpful and engaging notes you've been writing and filing away in a sensible place for the last year and a half? Well, now's the time to go back to them all and see what you've got to work with.

## Gather Your Notes and Look For Any Gaps

1) It's a good idea to start your revision for a subject by compiling all the notes you have for each topic. Don't worry if you haven't been filing away your notes as efficiently as you could have been — there's still time to get things in order. Dedicate some time to sorting through and organising everything before you get into the thick of your revision — it will save time later on.

2) Once you have a set of organised notes, check them against the course specification to make sure they cover everything. The spec shows you all the material you could be tested on in the exam.

3) It might help to print off a copy of the spec and tick off each point that you've got notes for. If you find something you've missed, make a note of it on the spec so that you know to come back to it.

## Fill in the Gaps by Adding to Your Notes

When you've read through the spec, go back and add to your notes until you've covered everything you need. The way you do this will depend on the subject, but here are some ideas:

### Use a textbook or a revision guide

- Textbooks and revision guides are designed to cover all the material in the spec. You could start by checking out CGP's cracking A-Level range...

- Use the books to fill in any gaps in your notes and check your understanding. Even if the information in the book is already in note form, making your own notes will help to consolidate your knowledge.

### Use the Internet or ask your teachers

- If you search online, make sure you use reliable sources. Asking your teachers to recommend useful websites or other sources can help you find the most appropriate information.

- Your teachers may also be able to help you by explaining any concepts you find difficult.

## Do one last check to make sure you haven't      any gaps in      notes...

Once you've made any extra notes, it's worth going back through the spec one more time. Knowing that you have notes that cover all the course content will give you confidence going into the next stage of your revision.

# Condensing Your Notes

Having a complete set of notes is a great feeling, but don't stop just yet — it's time to condense them...

## Pick Out the Key Information

1) The process of <u>simplifying your notes</u> will make you <u>actively engage with the content</u> and help to <u>reinforce the key information</u>. You'll also be left with a version of your notes that you can use to <u>quickly refresh your knowledge</u> of a topic without having to read through everything.

2) One of the simplest ways of condensing your notes is to write a <u>shortened version</u> of them on small <u>pieces of paper</u>, <u>cue cards</u> or <u>sticky notes</u>.

3) As you condense a set of notes, try to <u>reduce</u> any <u>detailed explanations</u> so that you're left with only the <u>key information</u>. If you <u>can't remember</u> the detailed explanation when you come to test yourself, you can always <u>look back at your full notes</u>.

Fluffy had condensed her notes into bitesized chunks.

**EXAMPLE:**

This is an example of how you could condense some English Literature notes about *The Great Gatsby* by F. Scott Fitzgerald onto a cue card.

Make sure each cue card has a clear heading — you may even want to number them.

### The Great Gatsby — Violence and Conflict in Relationships

- Most relationships in the novel are unhappy, unstable or violent — this is hinted at early on when two men carry their wives from Gatsby's garden "kicking, into the night".
- Women are treated as men's possessions — Tom gives Myrtle a dog leash, symbolising how he is in control of the affair. Tom decides when they meet and what Myrtle can say — he "broke her nose" for daring to say his wife's name.
- Tom and Gatsby argue over Daisy as if she's a possession and she has no autonomy.
- All of the marriages in the novel are unhappy. The characters' dissatisfaction with love leads to the violence that causes the death of three characters.
- Context — this could reflect Fitzgerald's own dissatisfaction and unhappiness with his marriage to Zelda. Their relationship was passionate, but filled with tension.

Use bullet points to keep your notes brief.

Use different colours to highlight different things (e.g. key words, quotes and context).

4) Your condensed notes will be a helpful <u>revision aid</u> in themselves, but it's definitely a good idea to produce <u>other revision aids</u> too (see p.28-31). These will help you to <u>reinforce your knowledge</u> and approach the content in <u>different ways</u> (e.g. you could create a mind map of the themes in *The Great Gatsby* and draw lines to connect similar ideas together).

## Don't try to condense your notes by just making the gaps between the letters smaller...

It can be tempting to write down every tiny bit of information when rewriting your notes, but remember that your condensed notes are designed to be concise and useful for revision, so try to be as selective as possible.

# Revision Techniques

The next four pages focus on the real bread and butter of revision — ~~eating snacks~~ revision techniques.

## Mind Maps are Great for Organising Information

1) The act of making a mind map can help you to <u>visualise information</u> and <u>identify links</u> between points.

2) Mind maps can also help you to <u>recall</u> key pieces of <u>information</u> in an exam if you're able to <u>picture</u> a specific mind map and what was written on it.

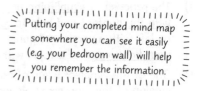

Putting your completed mind map somewhere you can see it easily (e.g. your bedroom wall) will help you remember the information.

**EXAMPLE:**

Here's an A-Level Geography mind map about desertification. You could add more detail (e.g. specific examples) to make it even more useful.

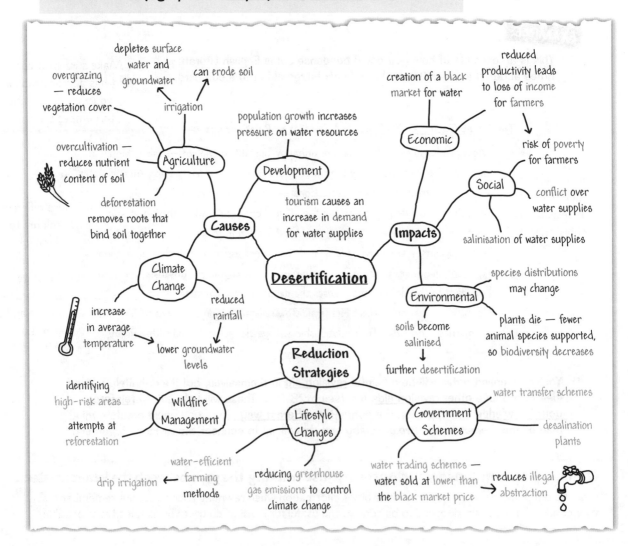

# Revision Techniques

## Use Flow Charts for Processes or Sequences

1)  You can use <u>flow charts</u> to revise anything that's split into a <u>series of steps</u>.

2)  They're useful for showing how different steps are <u>linked</u>, e.g. the order of events.

**EXAMPLE:**

Here's a flow chart that explains a thin-layer chromatography experiment for A-Level Chemistry.

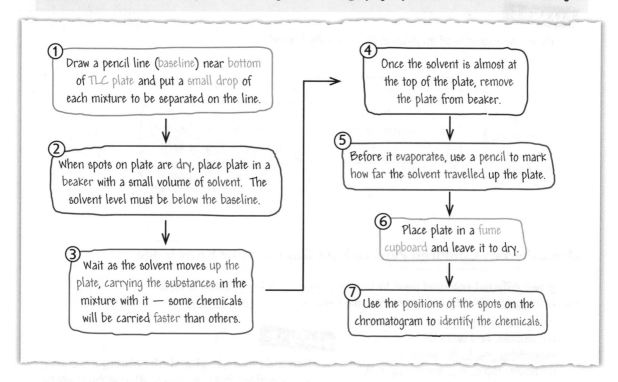

① Draw a pencil line (baseline) near bottom of TLC plate and put a small drop of each mixture to be separated on the line.

② When spots on plate are dry, place plate in a beaker with a small volume of solvent. The solvent level must be below the baseline.

③ Wait as the solvent moves up the plate, carrying the substances in the mixture with it — some chemicals will be carried faster than others.

④ Once the solvent is almost at the top of the plate, remove the plate from beaker.

⑤ Before it evaporates, use a pencil to mark how far the solvent travelled up the plate.

⑥ Place plate in a fume cupboard and leave it to dry.

⑦ Use the positions of the spots on the chromatogram to identify the chemicals.

## Have a go at Making Other Visual Aids

As well as mind maps and flow charts, you might want to make some other visual aids, including:

**Posters**

- Posters can be good for getting <u>lots of important information</u> about a topic down in <u>one place</u>.

- Like mind maps, it's a good idea to <u>stick them on your wall</u> when they're finished.

**Slide Shows**

- You can use a slide show to <u>present key information</u> or to <u>test yourself</u>.

- You can <u>edit information</u> easily and include revision <u>questions and answers</u> on subsequent slides.

Lauren's idea of turning herself into a visual aid wasn't working out as well as she'd hoped.

# Revision Techniques

## Make Flash Cards to Test Yourself

1) Flash cards are a great way of revising things like <u>key quotes</u>, <u>formulas</u>, <u>dates</u>, <u>terminology</u> and <u>vocabulary</u>.

2) <u>Making</u> the flash cards provides you with an opportunity to <u>go over the content</u>, and <u>testing yourself</u> with them (or getting someone else to test you) is a good way of checking that <u>everything has sunk in</u>.

Lucy was thrilled to receive her brother's old A-Level Economics flash cards for her birthday.

**EXAMPLE:**

Here's an example of an A-Level Business flash card.

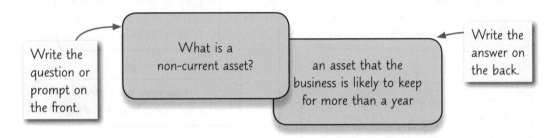

Write the question or prompt on the front.

What is a non-current asset?

an asset that the business is likely to keep for more than a year

Write the answer on the back.

## Use Different-Coloured Pens to Find Gaps in Your Knowledge

Using two different-coloured pens to test <u>how much you know</u> about a topic can help you to identify any areas you still need to <u>spend more time on</u>:

1) Set yourself a <u>time limit</u>, such as 15 minutes, and write down <u>everything you know</u> about a particular topic, e.g. by writing a <u>list of bullets</u> or drawing a <u>mind map</u>.

2) When <u>time has run out</u>, or you <u>can't think of anything else</u>, go back to your notes and use a <u>different-coloured pen</u> to add anything you <u>missed</u>.

3) By using different-coloured pens, you can easily identify the <u>material you've forgotten</u> or need to brush up on.

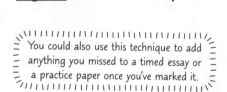
You could also use this technique to add anything you missed to a timed essay or a practice paper once you've marked it.

**EXAMPLE:**

Here's an example of part of a history mind map — everything in green was written without notes, and the information in red was added later.

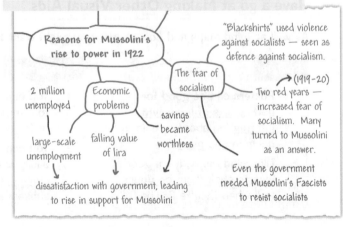

Reasons for Mussolini's rise to power in 1922

"Blackshirts" used violence against socialists — seen as defence against socialism.

The fear of socialism

(1919-20) Two red years — increased fear of socialism. Many turned to Mussolini as an answer.

2 million unemployed

Economic problems

savings became worthless

large-scale unemployment

falling value of lira

dissatisfaction with government, leading to rise in support for Mussolini

Even the government needed Mussolini's Fascists to resist socialists

# Revision Techniques

## Try Working With Others

While most of your time will be spent revising independently, varying your routine and working with others can help to keep things fresh (as long as you don't distract each other). You could:

Teach each other

Trying to explain a topic to someone else is a good way of testing how well you know it yourself.

Discuss ideas

You could share exam tips and strategies or pick a past paper question and discuss how you might answer it.

Test each other

Testing each other with quickfire questions in pairs or groups can be good for reinforcing information.

## Experiment With Some Memory Techniques

Sometimes it can help to use memory techniques to learn information. Here are some examples:

### Mnemonics

1) A mnemonic is a memory device where the first letters of the words you need to know become the first letters of a sentence, song or rhyme.

2) Mnemonics are especially useful for learning information in a certain order.

3) If you needed to remember Piaget's four stages of cognitive development (Sensorimotor, Preoperational, Concrete operational and Formal operational) for psychology, you could learn a silly mnemonic like 'Some Penguins Can Fly'.

### Memory Journeys

1) A memory journey is a way of linking landmarks on a journey with facts or words in a sequence.

2) For example, if you went on the same journey regularly, you could use wacky or creative links to associate each landmark with stages in a cycle or model.

3) For example, you could link each stage in the Park model of human response to natural disasters to a place on your regular walk to the shop. E.g. Phase One (Pre-disaster) — the opticians where you get your prescription. Phase Two (Disruption) — a pedestrian crossing that 'disrupts' your journey, etc.

---

**I love using memory techniques — my favourite one is... um... what was it again?**

You'll have used some revision techniques at GCSE, so think about which ones you found effective then.
You might need to adapt some of your techniques for A-Level though — don't be afraid to try something new.

# Alternative Revision Techniques

Sure — mind maps, flash cards and mnemonics are useful, but have you ever considered that there might be other revision techniques out there? If not, then reading these next two pages might just blow your mind...

## Get a Pet to Help You Revise

Revision is <u>tough</u>, so it's time to rope in Tiddles, Spot or Polly to help <u>take the weight off your shoulders</u>.

A rogue choice for a pet, but <u>bees</u> can be very helpful with <u>spelling practice</u>.

Make yourself <u>feel better</u> about your revision by <u>competing</u> with a <u>goldfish</u> to see who can remember the most answers in a set of <u>flash cards</u>.

<u>Parrots</u> are useful for <u>reinforcing key information</u> and learning <u>foreign languages</u> (they tend to be Polly-glots).

<u>Cats</u> are very good at <u>sitting on your work</u> — this will help to make sure you've got <u>all the key content covered</u>.

A <u>dog's</u> penchant for eating homework is unlikely to come in handy here, so why not teach them to <u>bring you snacks</u> instead? This works best with <u>retrievers</u> or <u>younger dogs</u>, as they're better at learning <u>new tricks</u>.

## Explore Your Passion for Dance

1) Learning to <u>express yourself</u> through dance could be the most important <u>disco(very)</u> of your revision period. Here are some <u>subject-specific ideas</u> to get you started:

Physics

Find a <u>partner</u> and practise some <u>lifts</u>, then work together to calculate the <u>forces</u> involved.

English Literature

Romeo-o-o, Romeo-o-o, Wherefore art thou Romeo-o-o...

Set some <u>key quotes</u> to <u>music</u>, then <u>dance</u> and <u>sing</u> it out.

History

Use the fact you're studying history as an <u>excuse</u> to <u>prance around</u> in <u>period dress</u>.

2) Another way of incorporating <u>dance</u> into your revision is to take up <u>tap dancing</u> — whenever you reach a <u>tricky topic</u> or are finding something <u>hard</u>, you can <u>stamp out</u> some of that frustration.

# Alternative Revision Techniques

## Build a Time Machine

This one's a bit of a <u>gamble</u> — get it <u>wrong</u>, and you've <u>wasted</u> all of your <u>revision time</u> dismantling an old washing machine and staining the carpet.  Get it <u>right</u>, and you've got <u>all the revision time in the world</u>...*

 **Think about the design**

- Are you going to use a <u>car</u>, a <u>bath tub</u>, a <u>toilet</u> or <u>something else</u>? Should you prioritise <u>style</u> or <u>function</u>?  It's best to sort this <u>early on</u>.

- Don't forget to leave some space for your <u>revision materials</u> — those A-Level Economics textbooks are heftier than you think.

> I think I'm going into a spin cycle!

 **Bring lots of snacks**

- You wouldn't want to end up in 1534 and realise you can't get any <u>digestives</u>, so <u>plan ahead</u>.

- Pack a <u>caesar salad</u> just in case you end up in <u>ancient Rome</u>.

**3** **Sort out the time travel bit**

- This is where things get a little... <u>tricky</u>.  I did figure it out, but I <u>forgot</u> to write everything down. It definitely involved a <u>screwdriver</u> and <u>a lot of gummy bears</u> though, so that's a <u>good place to start</u>...

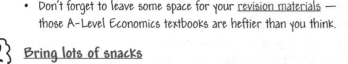

**EXAMPLE:**

My time machine was made out of an old sofa and a digital radio.  I finished building it next year.

> Be careful — try not to accidentally erase your own birth, get stuck in the Stone Age, or step on a butterfly and return to find you're studying a completely different set of A-Levels.

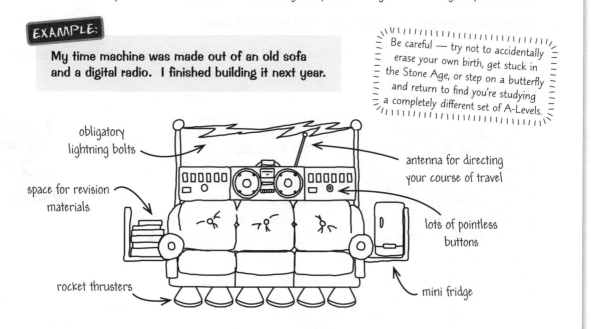

obligatory lightning bolts

antenna for directing your course of travel

space for revision materials

lots of pointless buttons

rocket thrusters

mini fridge

## Hello?  Can you hear me?  It's me from the future.  I've got some advice for you...

I've seen your future and it turns out that the stuff about exam practice on the next two pages is a lot more useful for your revision than all this stuff about dancing and time machines.  Sorry — hindsight is a wonderful thing...

*OK — you could just travel to the future and find out the exam answers, but that's no fun.

# Exam Practice

Once you've got a good understanding of the course content, it's time to put that knowledge into practice by focusing a bit more closely on the exams themselves. That's where these next two pages come in.

## The Best Way to Practise is to Simulate the Exam

1) A-Level exams don't just test your <u>knowledge</u> of a subject — they also test your ability to <u>apply that knowledge</u>.

2) That's why doing <u>practice papers</u> is really important — it's a great way of seeing how much you've <u>taken in</u>, while also practising how to <u>apply</u> what you've learnt.

3) Replicating <u>exam conditions</u> when you do these will help you get a feel for what it'll be like in the <u>actual exam</u>:

- Giving yourself the <u>same amount of time</u> you'll have in the exam will help you to practise your <u>time-management skills</u>.

- Answering the questions <u>without your notes</u> means you can see what material you've <u>learnt</u> and what you need to <u>revise again</u>.

4) Make the most of any <u>mock exam periods</u> and <u>revise for them</u> properly. This will allow you to <u>spot any issues</u> in your preparation (e.g. if you've focused too much on the earlier exams and not left enough time to revise for the later ones). You can then <u>improve your approach</u> before the <u>real exams</u>.

Ayah took simulating the exam environment to another level.

You should be able to find past papers on the exam board's website.

## Find Ways to Improve After You've Done a Paper

Don't put away a practice paper once you've finished it — use <u>these resources</u> to help you <u>improve</u>:

### Mark Schemes

- These give you the <u>correct answers</u> and show you how marks are <u>allocated</u>. <u>Checking your answers</u> against the mark scheme will help you to identify <u>questions you struggled with</u> and to work out what you could have <u>done better</u>.

- Mark schemes often want you to be <u>very specific</u> in your answer, e.g. to use <u>certain terminology</u> to get the mark. Looking through them will help you to identify what <u>information</u> you <u>need to put in your answers</u>.

- They also show you how many marks are given for each <u>assessment objective</u> in a question — this can help you to work out how much to focus on <u>each AO</u> in certain <u>question types</u>.

Mark's schemes were always purrfectly diabolical.

### Examiners' Reports

- These reports are written by the people who <u>mark the exams</u>, so they're full of <u>useful advice</u>, including what kind of answers were <u>successful</u> and what <u>mistakes</u> candidates often made.

- Use the <u>successes</u> and <u>mistakes</u> of past candidates to help guide your answers, including working out <u>what to focus on</u> and <u>what to avoid doing</u>.

If you notice something in a mark scheme or examiner's report that's missing from your notes, go back and add to them. You can also highlight any areas that you forgot or where you lost marks.

# Exam Practice

## You Can Practise in Smaller Chunks Too

If you <u>haven't got time</u> to do a full practice paper, or you want some <u>variety</u>, try these alternatives:

- For subjects where you'll need to write essays, you could <u>write</u> and <u>mark</u> some <u>individual essay questions</u>. You'll need to pay close attention to the <u>mark scheme</u> to estimate how many marks you might have got. Look at how many marks are allocated for each <u>assessment objective</u>, and think about whether you've <u>written enough</u> for each.

  If you're struggling, you could ask your teacher to read through an essay and give you some pointers for how you could improve.

- Try <u>swapping exam answers</u> or <u>essays</u> with a classmate so you can <u>give feedback</u> on each other's work and <u>share ideas</u>. This should help you to see what you <u>do well</u> and what you <u>need to work on</u>.

- You can also try just <u>planning essay questions</u> — doing this for a range of questions will help you to get better at <u>structuring essays quickly</u> and working out <u>what to cover</u>.

- Focus your time and attention on practice questions for the <u>topics you're struggling with</u> or the <u>question types you need to work on</u> (questions where you have to <u>apply your knowledge</u> can be especially tricky). If you answer lots of <u>similar questions</u>, you'll get a feel for how to do it <u>in the exam</u>.

## Don't Worry if You're Struggling at First

1) Having a go at practice papers can be <u>stressful</u>, especially if you're not doing as well as you'd like to, but try not to panic.

2) The <u>more practice</u> you do, the <u>more familiar</u> you'll become with what to expect in the exam — this should increase your <u>confidence</u> and make things feel <u>less frightening</u> on the day.

3) You might want to try sitting some practice papers <u>twice</u> — if you <u>struggled</u> with a paper, try <u>leaving a bit of time</u> and then <u>resitting it later</u> in the revision process. Hopefully, you'll have made some <u>encouraging progress</u>, which should help you to <u>feel better</u> about your revision.

"Doris, darling, look — I did much better this time!"

---

## Remember to always give 100% — unless you get a job as an examiner...

Sitting an A-Level exam without doing exam practice is like taking a driving test without ever having driven a car. You can read all about the subject as much as you like, but there's no substitute for practising the real thing.

# Looking After Yourself

A-Levels can be stressful, especially during the revision period, so it's important that you look after yourself. Look over these self-care tips — they should help you to avoid becoming too tired, stressed or overworked.

## Learn to Spot the Signs of Stress

1) While a little bit of stress can help to keep you focused and motivated, too much of it can have a negative impact on your health.

2) Knowing the signs of stress means you'll be able to notice them more easily — this will help you to realise when you (or one of your friends) need support:

> ### Possible signs of stress
>
> - A loss of appetite or overeating
> - Withdrawing from other people
> - Feeling anxious
> - Difficulty concentrating
> - Feeling more emotional than usual
> - Struggling to sleep

## It Can Be Helpful to Talk to People

1) If you ever feel too stressed, remember that you're not alone — talking to someone about how you feel can make things much better.

2) If you don't feel comfortable talking to friends, family or teachers, there are support services and helplines available where you can talk to someone confidentially.

3) BUT... Don't feel like you have to discuss revision or exams with friends and classmates if it causes you stress or makes you feel uncomfortable.

4) If you do talk about these things, try not to compare yourself to others too much. People often exaggerate how well things are going when it comes to exams and revision.

## Remember That Things Don't Always Go To Plan

1) Try not to worry if you don't manage to keep to your revision schedule or you don't feel like you're making as much progress as you'd like — it's important to accept that you're not going to be productive 100% of the time.

2) Try to avoid setting yourself unrealistic targets for the same reason — working in small, manageable chunks and taking regular breaks will help you keep motivated and stay positive (see page 10).

# Looking After Yourself

Here are some top ways of taking care of yourself — they're useful for life, not just the revision period.

## ① Try to maintain a regular sleep pattern

- Try to get <u>enough sleep</u>, especially if you've been revising for most of the day — sleeping helps you <u>remember</u> what you've learnt.

- Going to bed around the <u>same time</u> and setting an <u>alarm</u> for the next morning will help you to create a <u>consistent sleep routine</u>.

- Try to do something <u>relaxing</u> before bed, but it's best to <u>avoid looking at a screen</u>.

- Don't be tempted to <u>skip sleep</u> to revise — you might <u>struggle to concentrate</u> on what you're revising and you'll feel <u>tired</u> the next day.

## ② Eat a balanced diet and drink plenty of water

- Try to eat a <u>balanced diet</u> (that means not leaving your veggies) and avoid <u>skipping meals</u>. This will give you <u>energy</u> for revision and help you stay <u>healthy</u>.

- Make sure you drink <u>water</u> regularly to keep yourself <u>hydrated</u>.

## ③ Keep active and get some fresh air

- Going <u>outside</u> or <u>exercising</u> can be a really good way of <u>clearing your head</u>.

- This could be as simple as going for a <u>short walk</u> in your <u>revision breaks</u>.

## ④ Set time aside for relaxation or hobbies

- Taking some time to <u>relax</u> and doing something you <u>enjoy</u> — either on <u>your own</u> or <u>with friends</u> — can give you a much-needed break and stop you feeling <u>overwhelmed</u> by your work.

- Keep up some of your <u>hobbies</u> during the revision period. As with most things, it's important to find a <u>balance</u>.

## Exams are important, but your health should come first...

Looking after your health is really important if you want to do well in your exams. If you're feeling well-rested and healthy, you'll revise more productively, so don't think that giving yourself a well-earned break is wasted time.

# Maths and Further Maths

This next section is chock-full of study, revision and exam tips for a range of different A-Level subjects. If you like the sound of the equation *you + maths = success*, then these next pages are just for you.

## How Maths and Further Maths are Linked

I.   While some topics in A-Level Further Maths are completely new (e.g. complex numbers and matrices), most of them build on what you'll study in A-Level Maths.  If there's a Further Maths topic that requires knowledge from A-Level Maths, it will come at a point in the course where you already have this knowledge to build on.

2.   Although Maths and Further Maths are similar, it's important to keep your notes separate so you know which topics to revise for each exam — all the A-Level Maths questions will be answerable without Further Maths knowledge.

## Refresh Your Knowledge and Get Plenty of Practice

1)   Large parts of A-Level Maths build on the concepts you learnt at GCSE, so it's important to make sure you're familiar with everything you studied for GCSE Maths.

2)   Although A-Level Maths builds on your GCSE knowledge, there's plenty of new content to learn too — doing regular practice exercises is the best way to help you learn all the course content.

3)   You'll also be introduced to new mathematical notation at A-Level — make sure you understand how to use it correctly as it's important for picking up marks in the exam.

4)   Get familiar with your calculator — you'll need to do a range of things on it, including switching between degrees and radians, and using statistical functions.

## Understand How Mathematical Models and Proofs Work

Mathematical models and proofs come up in both Maths and Further Maths.

1)   Make sure you're able to turn real-life situations into mathematical models and can use models to solve problems.  The best way to do this is by practising questions that present different scenarios.

2)   You also need to be familiar with the language of proof — get in lots of practice at setting out a clear, logical argument to prove something. Speak to your teacher or look at a practice paper answer to see what you need to show in your proof to get marks in the exam — usually, answers to proof questions must be error-free to get full marks.

3)   In Further Maths, proof by induction has a clear, set structure to it. You need to learn this structure and stick to it when using this proof.

Mandy already knew that the proof was in the pudding.

# Maths and Further Maths

## Learn What You Need to Do for Different Questions

It can be tempting to read questions <u>quickly</u> in an exam, but it's important that you <u>follow the instructions exactly</u> so you do what's needed to <u>get the marks</u>. Here are some examples of <u>key words</u> you might see:

| Key Word | Meaning |
|---|---|
| Find / Calculate / Determine | Give an answer with working out |
| Prove / Show that | Use a logical argument to show why something is true or false |
| Plot | Mark points accurately on a graph |
| Sketch | Draw a diagram showing the main features of the graph |
| Exact | Give an exact answer with no rounding |
| Estimate | Give an approximate answer, but still show your working |
| Hence | Use the previous statement or question part to answer the next bit |

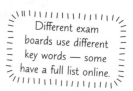

Different exam boards use different key words — some have a full list online.

## Get Familiar With the Large Data Set

1) Some <u>statistics</u> questions for A-Level Maths refer to the <u>large data set</u>.

2) The good news is that you're able to look at this data <u>before the exam</u> — it's likely you'll use it to <u>answer problems in class</u> and you can also <u>study it</u> in <u>your own time</u>. You don't have to learn the <u>precise data</u>, but you should have a <u>general understanding</u> of the data set as a whole.

## Know What's in Your Formula Booklet

You'll be given a <u>formula booklet</u> in the exam, so make sure you <u>know how to use it</u>:

### THE BIG BOOK OF FORMULAS

- You should <u>understand what every formula</u> in the booklet <u>means</u> and <u>how to use it</u>, — there's no point in having it if you can't apply it correctly.

- For the formulas and equations that <u>aren't</u> <u>included</u>, e.g. the quadratic formula, use <u>cue cards</u> or <u>other memory techniques</u> (see pages 28-31) to learn them.

Taylor had Formula One™ sorted, but she wasn't so sure about the other ones.

# Maths and Further Maths

## Show Your Working Out

1) Just like in GCSE Maths, it's important to <u>show your working out</u>. If you <u>don't get the correct answer</u>, you could <u>still get marks</u> for <u>showing your method</u>.

2) It can sometimes be helpful to use <u>diagrams</u> as part of your working out, particularly in <u>mechanics</u>. Diagrams can help you <u>visualise a problem</u> and <u>show the examiner</u> what you're trying to do.

3) Write <u>any formula</u> that you're going to use for a question, e.g. write $v = u + at$ before you use it. You can sometimes <u>grab a mark</u> for writing the <u>correct formula</u> out and then <u>using it</u>, even if you use it <u>incorrectly</u>.

Ryan's teacher was unimpressed with the lack of effort he put into working out.

## Use These Tips to Avoid Losing Marks

Where's that Mark gone...?

 Pay attention to the <u>units</u> used <u>in the question</u> — you'll sometimes be asked to <u>give your answer in one unit</u> (e.g. metres), but the question will give you the <u>information in a different unit</u> (e.g. centimetres).

 Check your answers for <u>silly mistakes</u> ($a^2 \times a^3$ is not $a^6$).

Where possible, check your answers by <u>working backwards</u>, e.g. putting your answer back into the equation to make sure it's correct.

 Check <u>how many marks</u> each question is worth and make sure you do enough work to get those marks.

 Write down a <u>decimal answer</u> in full <u>before rounding</u> it to what the question asks for. Avoid using a <u>rounded answer</u> in any further question parts unless you're told to do so.

 Look in your <u>pockets</u> — it's the first place I check for lost marks.

---

## I'll practise using formulas, but practising graphs is where I draw the line...

There's a lot to get your head around with Maths and Further Maths, but the most effective way to learn it all is by doing lots of practice. That way, you can see what you're comfortable with and work on things you find tricky.

# General Science Skills

These next pages are for things that crop up in all the science subjects.  Don't be shy — dive right in...

## Create Your Own Glossary of Terms

1) For each science subject you take, compile a list of scientific terms and their definitions — using mark schemes can be a good way of finding definitions that examiners like.

2) Refer to your glossary of terms throughout the course and during your revision.  This will help you get to grips with concepts and make sure you pick up marks for defining terms correctly in the exams.

Every entry Arthit added to his glossary was a defining moment in his chemistry revision.

## Practise Drawing Diagrams

1) Drawing a diagram can help to make a complicated concept easier to understand — for example, sketching a cross-section of an artery in your notes will help you to visualise any written explanation.

2) You can also use diagrams when it comes to revision — having one on a flash card can be a useful way of condensing a key concept.

3) Make sure you don't lose marks for drawing inaccurate diagrams in the exam — e.g. you shouldn't draw gases passing through straight lines.

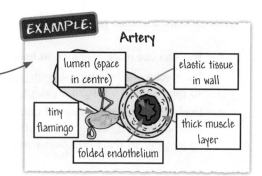

EXAMPLE:

Artery

lumen (space in centre)

elastic tissue in wall

tiny flamingo

thick muscle layer

folded endothelium

## You'll Need Good Practical Skills for Experiments and Exams

You'll do practical experiments in class, and you'll also be expected to apply practical skills and knowledge to experimental contexts in the exams:

Always follow general lab safety procedures and any safety instructions your teacher gives you carefully.

### During the Course

- You'll know some of the details beforehand, but you should look over related bits of theory before any of your practicals.

- You can find videos of experiments on the internet to give you an idea of what to expect — just be aware that the explanations might not be A-Level specific and the method may not be the one you'll be using in class.

- Don't worry too much if a practical goes wrong — you should get several chances to do each experiment.

### For the Exams

- It's unlikely that you'll have to do a practical during your exams, but you'll definitely be asked questions about experiments.

- The questions might be about similar practicals to ones you've done in class, or they might be about unfamiliar experiments.

- To answer these questions, you'll have to apply your knowledge of practical skills.  Make sure you go over your notes to re-familiarise yourself with experimental processes.

# General Science Skills

## Don't Forget to Work on Your Maths Skills

1) You'll need good <u>maths skills</u> for all the science subjects (e.g. for <u>solving calculations</u> and <u>analysing data</u>), so make sure you spend some time <u>practising</u> them, especially if you're not doing <u>A-Level Maths</u>.

2) To give your maths skills a <u>boost</u>, consider using some <u>learning resources</u> that focus specifically on using <u>maths skills in science</u>.

*You could start by checking out CGP's Essential Maths Skills for A-Level Science range.*

## Mark Schemes Can Help Tailor Your Revision

Science mark schemes give <u>precise details</u> and can be <u>very specific</u> about how marks are earned.

- You can use mark schemes to help <u>condense your notes</u> to just the <u>key points</u>.
- Mark schemes tell you the <u>precise terminology</u> you need to use to get marks, so they're a <u>useful tool</u> for <u>learning key terms</u>.
- Some mark schemes also tell you what <u>won't be accepted</u> in an answer — knowing what to <u>avoid</u> can often be just as helpful as knowing what to <u>include</u>, so don't skip over these comments in mark schemes.

*Don't forget to look at examiners' reports too (see p.34).*

## Practise Applying Your Scientific Knowledge

1) In the exam, you'll be presented with questions set in <u>unfamiliar contexts</u>. To answer these, you'll need to <u>apply what you've learnt</u> during the course.

2) A good way to get better at applying your knowledge is by doing <u>practice questions</u> — this will <u>improve your ability</u> to <u>identify what area</u> of the subject a <u>question</u> is <u>testing you on</u>.

3) As you go through the course, think about how content, practical techniques and mathematical techniques from <u>different topics link together</u> — this will enhance your <u>understanding of the subject</u> and make it easier to <u>apply your knowledge</u> to <u>different areas</u>.

Hetty realised fairly early on that she was being tested on her understanding of waves.

---

## I'm still sad this page isn't about Sergeant Science Skills...

If you have to do maths in a science exam, be careful with units. If the question tells you which units to give your answer in, don't throw away marks by giving it in different ones. As with all subjects, read the questions carefully.

# Biology

Biology is great because it focuses on the really vital things — how our hearts work, the structure of DNA and, most importantly, how to be a fun guy. Oh, sorry, that's fungi. Still important, I guess...

## You Need to Learn About **Structures** and **Functions**

You'll need to know what various biological structures <u>look like</u> and <u>how they work</u>.
Luckily for you, there are a number of good ways to learn about their <u>properties</u>:

When you come across a <u>new structure</u>, e.g. of a mitochondrion, draw a <u>labelled diagram</u> of it on a <u>flash card</u>.

For more <u>detailed structures</u>, e.g. a prokaryotic cell, try drawing a <u>labelled diagram</u> in the middle of a piece of paper. Then, write <u>information</u> about the structure <u>around the outside</u>.

To help you remember the properties of something, e.g. of water, try <u>summarising</u> them as a <u>numbered list</u>. Knowing that there are a <u>certain number</u> can <u>jog your memory</u>.

## Make Sure You Understand **Biological Processes** and **Cycles**

1) <u>Processes</u> and <u>cycles</u> are a key part of biology — they can add up to <u>a lot of marks</u> in the exams because they crop up in many <u>different questions</u>.

2) <u>Flow charts</u> are a really good way of learning processes and cycles (see page 29). You can <u>condense</u> them into steps and put each step in its own box. This can help you <u>visualise the process</u> more clearly and <u>remember the correct order</u> of the steps.

3) You could also use a <u>mnemonic</u> or <u>acronym</u> to help you remember each stage. E.g. you could remember '<u>I</u> <u>P</u>refer <u>M</u>y <u>A</u>pples <u>T</u>art' or <u>IPMAT</u> for the stages of the cell cycle (<u>I</u>nterphase, <u>P</u>rophase, <u>M</u>etaphase, <u>A</u>naphase and <u>T</u>elophase).

## Practise Using **Statistical Tests**

1) <u>Practical skills</u> are important in A-Level Biology — you'll do <u>practicals in class</u> and <u>answer questions</u> about practical skills in <u>the exam</u>. As part of this, you'll need to use <u>statistical tests</u> to <u>analyse data</u>.

2) A range of <u>statistical tests</u>, such as the <u>chi-squared test</u>, can crop up in both practicals and the exam.

3) You need to know how to <u>use</u> these different tests and how to <u>select the correct one</u> to use.

4) Once you're familiar with <u>how</u> and <u>when</u> each statistical test is used, having a go at some <u>practice questions</u> will help you to <u>apply this knowledge</u> to <u>new contexts</u>.

---

### These tips will set you on the path to ex-cell-ent results in your exams...

Try adding doodles to your notes or revision aids to help you remember the key features of something. E.g. draw a person running beside processes that require energy from ATP, and a person lying down next to passive processes.

# Chemistry

It's safe to say that revision and exam preparation are key substances in any successful chemistry mixture. To find out how to create the perfect formula for A-Level Chemistry bliss, cast your eyes over this page.

## Learn the Correct Conventions

1) Chemistry has <u>lots of rules</u> and <u>conventions</u> that need to be followed, e.g. <u>using square brackets</u> for concentrations and <u>curly arrows</u> to show the movement of a pair of electrons in a <u>mechanism</u>.

**EXAMPLE:**

This mechanism shows how chloromethane reacts with a hydroxide ion to form methanol and a chloride ion.

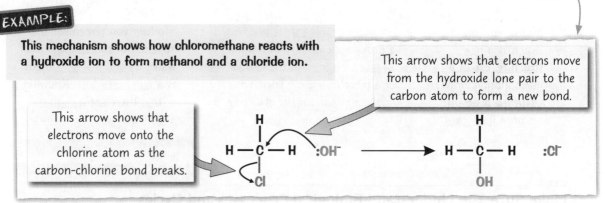

This arrow shows that electrons move from the hydroxide lone pair to the carbon atom to form a new bond.

This arrow shows that electrons move onto the chlorine atom as the carbon-chlorine bond breaks.

2) Speak to your <u>teacher</u> about <u>best practices</u> and make sure you know all the <u>right conventions</u> so that you don't end up <u>losing marks</u> in the exam.

## Learn Rules to Help You Save Time

1) There are a few <u>rules</u> that can <u>save you time</u> when you're revising the course content.

2) For example, you can use the number of <u>bonding</u> and <u>lone electron pairs</u> on the <u>central atom</u> of a molecule to predict the <u>shape of that molecule</u>.  This means you <u>don't have to memorise</u> the shape of lots of different molecules.

3) Try to make a note of <u>useful rules like this</u> throughout the course.

## Practise Answering Multiple-Choice Questions

A  <u>Most exam boards</u> include a multiple-choice question section on <u>at least one paper</u> — check if yours does.

B  Even if you think you know the <u>answer</u> to a question, it's worth going through the <u>other options</u> in turn and checking that <u>none of them could be correct</u>.

C  If there's a multiple-choice question you <u>can't answer</u>, just have a <u>guess</u>.  Try to <u>rule out any wrong answers</u> first though.

Herbert had been making difficult choices for as long as he could remember.

# Physics

If you're feeling the full force (N) of physics, then having a good read of the tips on this page might just help to lessen the mass (kg) on your shoulders and get your velocity (ms⁻¹) moving in a positive direction.

## Practise Using and Rearranging Formulas

1) Make your own <u>list of formulas</u> as you go through the course. <u>Label the letters and variables</u> to show what they <u>represent</u> and what <u>units</u> they use — this will <u>reinforce your understanding</u> of each formula and when to use it.

2) Practise solving simultaneous equations and <u>rearranging formulas for different variables</u> — this comes up a lot in exams.

3) When you're <u>using formulas for calculations</u>, get into the habit of <u>writing out the following steps</u>:

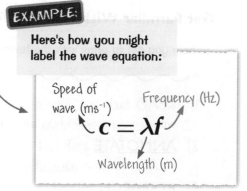

EXAMPLE:

Here's how you might label the wave equation:

Speed of wave (ms⁻¹)    Frequency (Hz)

$$c = \lambda f$$

Wavelength (m)

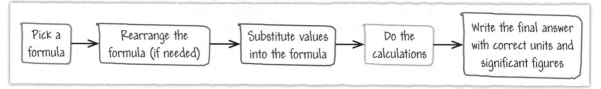

Pick a formula → Rearrange the formula (if needed) → Substitute values into the formula → Do the calculations → Write the final answer with correct units and significant figures

## Be Sure to Brush up on Your Maths Skills

1) <u>Lots of the marks</u> up for grabs in A-Level Physics will <u>require maths skills</u>, so make sure you <u>know your stuff</u>.

2) Get to know your <u>calculator</u> and how to get to the different functions you'll need <u>quickly</u>, so you don't <u>waste time</u> in the exam.

3) If you're stuck, look back at <u>previous parts</u> of the question to see if there's any <u>other information</u> that can help you.

4) Use <u>unrounded values</u> throughout your <u>working out</u> and only round your answer <u>at the end</u>.

In calculation questions, you should always show your working — you may get some marks for your method even if you get the answer wrong.

### Significant Figures

- Give your answer to the <u>same number of significant figures</u> (SFs) as the <u>piece of data with the fewest SFs</u> that you've used in your calculation, e.g. when given $v = 1.532$ and $t = 0.91$, your answer should be two SFs.

- The <u>exception</u> is when you're asked to 'show that' a <u>variable equals a value</u>, e.g. $s = 1.4$ m. In these cases, your answer should be <u>one more significant figure</u> than the <u>quoted figure</u>.

## The fun you can have with physics is always rising at an exponential rate...

Chances are you'll have to answer some multiple-choice questions in one or more of your physics exams, so make sure you practise answering these. Take a look at the bottom of the previous page for some more advice.

# English Literature

To do well in English Literature, you need to have a firm understanding of the texts — who wrote them, what messages they're trying to convey, what their favourite takeaway meal is. It's all really important stuff...

## Get Familiar With Your Set Texts

To help you get to grips with the texts you're studying, you should:

1) <u>READ</u> each text <u>numerous times</u> — leaving a gap between readings will <u>stimulate new ideas</u> and help you <u>draw connections between texts</u>.

2) <u>ANNOTATE</u> each text — if you <u>add notes each time you read</u> a text, you'll build up a <u>bank of notes</u> that you can use to help you revise.

3) <u>RESEARCH</u> beyond the texts themselves — talking about <u>context</u> can be worth <u>big marks</u>, and engaging with <u>literary criticism</u> will help to open up <u>different ways of thinking</u> about a text.

4) <u>WATCH</u> adaptations — <u>seeing a text performed</u> as a film, television programme or play can help you <u>visualise key moments and characters</u>.

> If you're allowed to take a copy of the text into your exam, you'll need to make sure you have a clean version without notes.

## Get Familiar With Literary Devices and Theories

1) You'll be expected to <u>pick out and analyse literary devices</u> in a text, so it's important that you know a <u>range of techniques</u> and understand <u>why a writer might use them</u>.

2) It's also a good idea to learn about <u>literary theories</u> (e.g. feminist or Marxist theory) — these can lead to <u>new ways of analysing texts</u> and can be used to <u>back up your points</u> in the exam.

3) If you're unsure about literary devices and theories, <u>ask your teacher for help</u>. Once you're confident with them, applying them to texts will be a lot easier.

## Practise Comparing Texts

1) Part of your A-Level is assessed on your ability to <u>compare and contrast texts</u> through their use of things like language, structure and form.

2) Practise comparing your set texts as well as <u>unseen texts</u> — <u>read a range</u> of short stories and poetry, then try <u>drawing connections</u> between the texts you've read. You could do this by listing comparisons in a <u>notebook</u> or by making a <u>visual aid</u>, such as a mind map or Venn diagram.

3) You can even try comparing <u>other types of media</u>, e.g. two films. While this won't be as helpful as comparing literary texts, it will get you in the habit of <u>identifying shared themes and ideas</u>.

Lola was great at comparing the symbolism of emojis in different texts.

# English Literature

## Use Cue Cards to Learn Key Quotes

1) Focus on <u>memorising versatile quotes</u> that you'll be able to use in a <u>variety of essay questions</u>.

2) You can <u>organise your cards</u> in different ways, e.g. you might decide to do a set of cards for <u>each chapter</u> as you're working through the text, then make a set of cards for <u>each character or theme</u> and write a <u>short explanation</u> on the back that <u>links the quote back to the category</u>.

3) Even if your exams are <u>open book</u>, it's still important to learn quotes as it will <u>save you time</u> in the exams.

It's important to learn the names of authors, texts and characters — make sure you can spell them correctly.

*Oranges Are Not the Only Fruit*
by Jeanette Winterson

'I love you almost as much as I love the Lord.'

Romance and Love
Shows Jeanette's belief that her love for Melanie is not sinful — she believes it is not opposed to her love for God.

## Give Detailed Analysis in the Exam

It's important to <u>engage with the literature critically</u> and <u>explain your points</u> in detail rather than just describing what happens in the texts.

Talk about <u>literary devices</u> and <u>theories</u>, but <u>don't use them</u> when they're <u>not relevant</u> — examiners want to see that you can use them to say something about the <u>meaning</u> of the text.

Make sure that you're <u>answering the question</u>. It's very easy to go off on a tangent and discuss something you know rather than <u>applying your knowledge</u> to <u>what the question is actually asking you</u>.

For each paper, learn the weightings of the <u>assessment objectives</u> (AOs). In an English Literature answer, you're likely to cover <u>multiple AOs</u> in the <u>same point</u>, but you still need to make sure you're <u>not focusing too much</u> on a particular assessment objective throughout your answer.

## Learn your texts inside out — it'll put you in the examiner's good books...

It's likely that you'll spend a lot of time reading the same texts over and over again. To help you stay focused, try re-reading a text with a particular theory or theme in mind — this can help you to find new angles for analysis.

# English Language

As you know, English Language is more scientific than a lot of people realise. It involves collecting and analysing data, as well as applying linguistic theories. Here are some tips to set you on the path to success.

## Read or Listen to a Variety of Texts

Analysing a variety of spoken or written texts will help you to develop your ability to think critically about how writers and speakers attempt to convey meaning. Here are some ideas to get you started:

 Find a range of different texts to analyse — think about the purpose of each text and the context in which it was made. Then, think about how language has been used to support this purpose (see below).

 Find two texts on a similar topic and think about how they use language differently. E.g. you could find two different articles about the same news story, or compare a modern text to an older one and look out for ways that language use has changed over time.

Find examples of child language online. Think about how the language features each child uses reflect their age and how the child is attempting to communicate meaning.

Listen to famous people speaking (e.g. in interviews or online recordings). As you listen, think about how the person's use of language reflects their identity. You should consider factors like their age, background, dialect, gender and opinions, as well as when the recording was made.

## Get to Grips With Language Features

1) Before you analyse a text, it can help to jot down a list of the different language features you could look at.

2) Try creating a mnemonic to keep them lodged in your brain (see page 31). My personal favourite is "People Love Gloria's Pet DRAGon."

Phonetics, phonology and prosodics

Lexis and semantics

Grammar (morphology and syntax)

Pragmatics

Discourse

Register

Audience

Graphology

 This list is just an example — you might prefer to come up with your own.

It's tricky to write about things like lexis and syntax if you don't know what they mean, so try to learn all the linguistic terminology as early as possible. Making quizzes or writing flash cards are both good ways of making sure words like "semantics" actually mean something to you — see what I did there...

It's important to use these features to analyse meaning or to comment on the context of a text rather than just spotting that they've been used.

# English Language

## Make Sure Your Language Investigation is Accurate and Methodical

1) Most exam boards expect you to do some form of <u>language investigation</u> or <u>research project</u> as part of your A-Level.

2) Think about which <u>topics</u> you're interested in as you go through the course so that you have <u>some ideas</u> when you start the project.

3) The language investigation is a good opportunity to pick up <u>valuable marks</u> before the exams. In order to do well, you'll need to:

- Collect data accurately and think about the <u>limitations</u> of this data.
- Research studies with a <u>similar focus</u> to your investigation.
- Keep a <u>record</u> of your <u>sources</u> so you can <u>reference</u> studies.

Grace's friends were concerned that she was taking the 'investigation' side of the project a little too far.

## Focus on These Key Exam Tips

Getting lots of <u>practice</u> analysing texts will put you in a good place for exam success, but it's also <u>vital</u> to work on your <u>exam technique</u>. Remember to keep your answers focused on <u>language analysis</u>:

- Keep the <u>exam question</u> in mind at all times. It's easy to go <u>off on a tangent</u>, so make sure you write <u>specifically</u> about the use of language <u>in relation to the question</u> you've been asked.

- Make sure you go into the exam with a good understanding of all the <u>key linguistic theories</u>. Then, when you've read an exam question, you can write down a quick <u>list</u> of any <u>relevant theories</u> next to the question and <u>tick them off</u> as you include them in your answer.

- Make sure you're <u>familiar</u> with the <u>specification</u> and <u>exam structure</u> before you go into the exam. If you understand the <u>assessment objectives</u> and know how they're weighted, you'll know which <u>aspects of language use</u> to focus on in each paper.

- If you're <u>struggling</u> to analyse a text in the exam, don't be tempted to <u>paraphrase</u> the text — remember that you're analysing the <u>language</u> of the text, not <u>describing</u> what is happening. You should be wary of focusing too heavily on <u>graphology</u> for the same reason.

---

**I can only ever remember 25 letters in the English Language. I don't know 'y'...**

Some exam boards require you to write your own text. To help with this, practise writing different kinds of texts. As with analysing texts, you'll need to think about different language features and what effect they have.

# History

A-Level History isn't easy, so read these tips to make sure you don't end up on the wrong side of it...

## Get Familiar with Sources and Interpretations

You'll have already worked with sources and interpretations at GCSE, but it's important to spend some of your study time <u>analysing</u> and <u>comparing</u> different <u>sources and interpretations</u> related to your topics:

### Sources

Sources are pieces of <u>contemporary evidence</u>. When analysing a source's <u>usefulness</u>, think about its:

- <u>content</u> — <u>what</u> the source can <u>tell you</u> about the topic you're studying
- <u>provenance</u> — <u>who</u> made it, <u>where</u>, <u>when</u> and <u>why</u> (and how this <u>affects the content</u>)
- <u>accuracy</u> — whether the content <u>fits</u> with your <u>knowledge</u> of the topic

### Interpretations

Thinking about different <u>historical perspectives</u> is especially important at A-Level. You'll have to assess the <u>validity</u> of some <u>historians' interpretations</u> in the exam, so make sure you understand the main <u>historical debates</u> surrounding each topic.

Onwards — to exam VICtory!

## Practise Debating Important Issues

I put the VIII in historical debate...

1) A-Level History is all about <u>weighing up different factors</u> and forming <u>logical arguments</u> to support your interpretation.

2) To help you do this in your <u>essays</u>, it's important that you understand the <u>key historical debates</u> covered in your course.

3) In your essays, you must consider <u>both sides of the argument</u>. It's a good idea to fully explain the <u>arguments against your interpretation</u>, then go through and <u>critique each point</u> to show why your interpretation is <u>more valid</u>. To help with this, make sure you <u>listen to other people's arguments</u> when debating. You could also practise by debating in favour of an <u>argument you don't agree with</u>.

4) Here are some ideas for how you could <u>practise debating</u>:

| | | |
|---|---|---|
| Encourage debate within your <u>history class</u>. If you get involved in the <u>class discussion</u>, others are more likely to join in, making the lesson <u>more productive</u>. | Find one or more <u>classmates</u> to debate with outside of class. Give yourselves some time to do some <u>research</u>, then take it in turns to <u>make your case</u>. | When you're on your own, try making a <u>list of arguments for and against</u> a historical interpretation. If you're struggling, go and do <u>more research</u>. |

# History

## Dedicate Plenty of Time to Your Coursework

Whether you call it coursework, non-exam assessment or something else, you'll need to <u>research</u> and <u>write</u> an <u>extended essay</u> at some point during your course.  Here are some tips to help you ace it:

- <u>Plan your time</u> — break the project down into <u>separate stages</u>, then make a <u>timetable</u> or <u>checklist</u> with the different stages mapped out.  Assigning a <u>rough deadline</u> to each stage will help you stay <u>on track</u>.

- <u>Spend some time deciding on your question</u> — once you've decided which <u>topic</u> you want to focus on, look into it in more depth so that you can come up with a question that allows you to explore a <u>range of interpretations</u> in a <u>balanced way</u>.  Make sure you have enough <u>resources</u> to properly tackle your chosen question too.

- <u>Do lots of secondary reading</u> — the more <u>reading</u> you do, the more <u>material</u> you'll have to work with in your essay and the more <u>informed</u> your answer will be.  See pages 22-23 for some more detailed advice.

- <u>Make a detailed plan and write multiple drafts</u> — use the advice on pages 18-21 to help you write your essay.

## There's More to Revision Than Learning Facts

1) Knowing <u>facts</u>, <u>dates</u> and <u>statistics</u> will only be useful if you can <u>apply them</u> to an argument — it's no use knowing that the British Army suffered 300 000 casualties at the Battle of Passchendaele if you can't put this number <u>into context</u> and use it to <u>support your argument</u>.

2) To help you do this, try identifying the <u>key arguments for and against</u> a historical viewpoint, then write down a few facts and statistics that <u>support each argument</u>.  This will help you to learn the <u>significance</u> of each fact and statistic.

3) You can use a <u>range of techniques</u> to help you remember these facts (see pages 28-31).  For example, if you struggle to remember historical dates, you could create a <u>timeline</u> or try making up <u>rhymes</u> to help you, e.g. "1924 — Vladimir Lenin is no more".

4) The key thing to remember is that your answer should be an <u>argument</u>, <u>not a narrative</u>, so don't present <u>evidence</u> without any <u>analysis</u>.  The examiners will be more impressed if you can use a few pieces of <u>key information</u> in an <u>analytical way</u> than if you can reel off a <u>long list of facts</u>.

Betty loved historical dates so much, she started asking people out on them.

## Make sure it's your achievements — not your grades — that go down in history...

Whenever you revise a historical event or development, try to form a judgement about it — think about whether it was a success or failure and what consequences it had.  This will help to check you've understood the content.

# Geography

Ah, geography... From map reading and fieldwork to data analysis and essay writing, there's a lot more to it than just doing a bit of colouring in. Here are some tips to help you sharpen your geography skills.

## Follow These Tips Throughout the Course

Read the news to stay up to date with any world events that might be relevant to your course. Significant global events can happen at any time and reading about them might provide you with some relevant examples to use in the exam.

It's important to use the right terminology, so keep a glossary of all the key terms you come across. This will make it easy to look up a term you can't remember or check the meaning of a term. You'll also have a handy resource ready for when you start revising.

Practise analysing data from graphs, tables, charts, maps and other sources to familiarise yourself with different ways of presenting data. Make sure you can identify any trends and know how to spot any anomalies.

Dedicate a bit of time every week to improving your map-reading and interpretation skills. Find some maps with attached data sets (e.g. in journal articles, news reports or past papers), then practise analysing them. Make sure you can use a map to explain locations and landforms too.

Spend some time working on your maths skills, especially if you're not doing maths at A-Level. Some of the maths skills you need will be familiar from GCSE, but you may also come across some new concepts like standard deviation and Spearman's Rank correlation coefficient. Take the time to practise these skills and make sure you understand how to interpret the results.

Try to keep a clear and comprehensive set of notes for everything you learn in class. This is especially important for case studies — try to add more detail from your own research to your notes on these.

# Geography

## Make Sure You Plan Your Independent Fieldwork Investigation

1) <u>Researching</u> and <u>writing</u> an investigation from scratch can be a <u>lengthy process</u>, so it's a good idea to <u>plan</u> how you're going to use your time.

2) Break the project down into <u>stages</u>, from <u>deciding on a research question</u> all the way through to <u>making final tweaks</u> to your last draft. Make a checklist of these stages, with dates by which you'll have finished each one — you can then <u>tick off each stage</u> when you've completed it.

3) As part of the investigation, you'll need to carry out some <u>fieldwork</u>, <u>record</u> your findings, <u>present</u> them, <u>interpret</u> them and write a <u>report</u> outlining the whole investigation. Make sure you leave yourself <u>enough time</u> for each stage.

4) Even if you collect your field data as part of a <u>group</u>, your investigation is <u>independent</u>, so you need to <u>work on your own</u> when deciding on a research question, analysing your results and writing your report.

I think I've found a geyser!

Although you'll be collecting your own data, don't forget to use secondary data sources (such as journal articles or online data) in your project — it will help to strengthen your conclusions.

## Keep Your Exam Answers Focused on the Question

You're more likely to get high marks in the exams if you can <u>apply your knowledge</u> to answer the questions rather than just writing down everything you know about a topic or case study.

If you're using details from a <u>case study</u> to support your points in a longer answer, make sure the case study is <u>relevant</u> to the question — if you're writing about ecological succession in the <u>UK</u>, bringing in details from the <u>Amazon</u> won't cut it.

If you're given <u>a source</u>, analyse it closely and refer to it <u>specifically</u> in your answer. However, don't fall into the trap of trying to <u>explain</u> a set of data if the question doesn't ask you to.

Lou and his classmates had plenty of practice getting out of the examiners' traps.

If a question asks you to <u>what extent you agree</u> with a particular view, make sure you write about <u>both sides</u> of the argument. Finish with a <u>clear conclusion</u> that sums up how far you agree with the view.

## Someone asked if my mum likes geography puns. I said, "Alaska"...

Learning your case studies and being able to apply what you know will help you to get top marks in the exams. Use flash cards, mind maps or whatever works best for you to make sure you know all the facts for each one.

# Languages

The best way of improving your language skills is to get as much practice throughout the course as possible. Then, just add in a healthy dollop of exam technique, et voilà — you'll be well on the way to exam success.

## Keep Learning Vocab Throughout the Course

1) Find out the themes you'll be tested on in the exams and focus on learning vocab that's specifically related to these themes. It's important not to leave this too late — you won't be able to cram it all before the exams.

2) When you're preparing for the speaking exam, try to memorise some useful phrases or bits of vocab related to your individual research project. It will really help in the discussion if you can bring in relevant terminology or show off some impressive grammatical constructions.

3) One of the simplest ways of learning vocab is to use flash cards (see p.30), but it's also a good idea to keep a vocab book for new words you learn. There are plenty of websites and apps to help with learning vocab too — some allow you to make electronic flashcards and play recordings of each word in the foreign language to help you with listening and speaking practice.

Max could say 'I love chicken' in 17 languages.

## It's Important to Practise Your Foreign Language Regularly

Here are the main skills you'll need — you might want to focus on the ones you find trickiest:

### Speaking

The more you practise speaking in the target language, the easier it will be to keep talking in the speaking exam, so get into the habit of speaking to people (e.g. your classmates or language teachers) in the language whenever you can. You could even record yourself and listen back to it, e.g. when preparing phrases for the speaking exam.

### Reading

Read some short news articles or opinion pieces in your target language. It's best to read something related to one of the themes you're studying, so that you can impress the examiner with your up-to-date knowledge.

### Listening

Listen to music in your target language and take some time to look up the meaning of the lyrics. Watching foreign films or TV shows can also be a fun way of breaking up your study. If possible, watch with subtitles in the target language, but if you use English subtitles, make sure you pay attention to the original dialogue.

### Translation

Find some sentences or texts (in English or the target language) from a news article, blog, magazine or textbook, and try translating them without a dictionary. Then, go back and correct your mistakes using a dictionary and your grammar notes. If there are any grammar points you're unsure on, spend some time focusing on these.

# Languages

## Make Sure You Know Your Set Texts Really Well

1) Do some extra reading about the text(s) you're studying. You could read extracts from other works by the same author, watch more films by the same director, or read articles about the text(s) in the target language or English. It will help you stand out if you can show the examiner you've really engaged with your text(s).

2) Learning some specialist vocab related to literature or film will help when you have to write essays on your set text(s) in the exam. It's also a good idea to memorise a few short but versatile quotes from your text(s) as well as some useful phrases related to the author or director's techniques.

3) Occasionally, you could focus your speaking or translation practice on your set text(s) too — e.g. have a discussion about a text with one of your classmates or set yourself an extract to translate.

## Consider How You'll Approach the Exams

1) If you have an exam that involves listening, reading and writing in the same paper, think about which bits you're going to tackle first and which bits you're going to leave until the end.

2) When tackling listening questions, try not to panic. If you take the first questions slowly and listen to them a few times, you'll ease yourself in and relax a bit, giving yourself the best chance of picking up marks in the rest of the listening section.

3) If you have time, read over any essays — you'll be marked on grammatical accuracy, and you're more likely to make mistakes when writing in a foreign language.

Cali found listening to the sounds of a Spanish beach a little too relaxing.

## Try Not to Panic When Translating Unfamiliar Words

1) If you come across an unfamiliar word when translating from the language:

| Think about the word's etymology — see if it's similar to any other words you know, either in English or another language. | Think about the context — you might be able to guess the meaning of the word based on the rest of the sentence. | If you're still unsure, make a sensible guess rather than leaving a blank space. |
|---|---|---|

What on earth is "ein Affe"?

2) When translating into the language, try to avoid translating word for word — if you don't know a word in your target language, see if you can convey the same meaning using words you do know.

## Isn't it fantastico when you can sprechen muchos langues?

In the speaking exam, there are little things you can do to sound more natural, like pausing in your target language rather than in English — you'll sound better if you fill gaps in your French oral exam with 'euh' instead of 'um'.

# Business

Succeeding at A-Level Business is all about taking the theories you learn and understanding how they work in practice. It's a shame that the same can't be said for my 'Introduction to Time Travel' course...

## Study How Real Businesses Operate

 ### 1 Learn how the course content applies to real businesses

- Spend some of your independent study time <u>researching</u> a range of <u>businesses</u> (e.g. sole traders, PLCs and charities). Try to <u>apply</u> what you've learnt in class to each business you read about.

- Studying these examples will help <u>prepare</u> you for <u>analysing unfamiliar businesses</u> in the exams.

### 2 Keep a note of useful examples

- Make <u>notes</u> on any <u>business examples</u> you find that might be useful for the exams. Working these examples into your answers will help to <u>demonstrate</u> your <u>business awareness</u> and might earn you some extra marks.

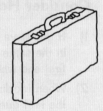

- Getting used to <u>discussing examples</u> also helps you to practise <u>applying your knowledge</u> to <u>specific businesses</u>, which will be helpful in the exams.

 ### 3 Use a variety of sources for your research

- Look up <u>specific businesses</u> that you know (e.g. visit <u>their website</u>) and follow <u>business news</u>.

- If you get the chance (e.g. if you have a relevant friend or family member), <u>talk to people</u> involved in <u>making business decisions</u>.

## Debate Business Questions

In the exams, you'll need to write answers that explore <u>both sides</u> of an <u>argument</u> in a <u>balanced way</u>. To practise doing this, you could try <u>debating</u> with a classmate or a family member:

1) Pick a <u>topic</u> and a <u>business</u>, then choose a <u>question</u>, e.g. "Should the business expand into a new market?".

2) Decide who is <u>for</u> and who is <u>against</u> the question. Take some time to <u>prepare your arguments</u>, then give yourselves time to make <u>clear, well-developed points</u> and to <u>ask or answer questions</u>. Once you've done, try to come to a <u>final judgement</u>.

3) You could turn it into a <u>game</u> by awarding <u>points</u> for things that will <u>earn you marks</u> in the exams, e.g. using <u>business terminology</u>.

The debate about whether alpacas were better than llamas hadn't gone as well as Hannah had hoped.

# Business

## Develop Your Maths Skills

1) You'll be expected to <u>do calculations</u> and <u>analyse data</u> in the exams, so practise doing this until you feel comfortable.

2) <u>Check</u> which <u>calculations</u> you might have to do in the exams (e.g. price elasticity, profit margins and exchange rates). Make a <u>list</u> of all these <u>calculations</u> so you can <u>tick off</u> each one when you're happy with it.

3) To help you get comfortable with these calculations, find some <u>business tools</u> (e.g. cash flow forecasts, budgets or statements of financial position) and practise <u>analysing</u> the <u>data</u> presented in them. Make sure you can read <u>pie charts</u>, <u>graphs</u> and <u>data tables</u> that might be used to present data.

Damian was always calculating how he could improve his market share.

## Learn All the Key Definitions and Theories

1) Knowing <u>definitions</u> of business terms will earn you marks in <u>multiple-choice questions</u> (if they're included in your exam), but you could also get marks for including them in <u>short-</u> and <u>longer-answer questions</u>. For example, if you're writing an essay about how a business could change its marketing mix, it's a good idea to <u>start by defining</u> what a marketing mix is.

2) Take the time to learn about the <u>key business models</u> so that you can refer to them in your answers when it's relevant. For example, if a question asks you to <u>assess</u> a business's decision to move into a new market, you could <u>describe</u> how Porter's Five Forces model could be used to consider how attractive the new market is.

## Know What to Expect From Different Exam Questions

### Learn the Command Words

- Questions which ask you to <u>describe</u>, <u>explain</u> or <u>calculate</u> test your business <u>knowledge</u> and your ability to <u>apply it</u>.

- Questions which ask you to <u>analyse</u> or <u>assess</u> want you to use your knowledge to <u>consider</u> different aspects of a topic or issue.

- Questions which ask you to <u>evaluate</u> want you to <u>make a judgement</u> and use your business knowledge to justify your opinion.

### Respond to Case Studies

- Use <u>specific facts</u> and <u>figures from the data</u> you've been given in any case studies to <u>back up</u> your arguments (as long as it's relevant to your answer).

- <u>Include some analysis</u> rather than just describing the data you're given, e.g. <u>make links</u> between different factors or discuss its significance.

## You'll want to make exam revision your business...

If you're doing a longer-answer question that involves evaluation, don't skip straight to the evaluation bit — you get marks for showing the different exam skills, so make sure that you include definitions and apply your knowledge.

# Economics

There are plenty of concepts, theories and formulas you'll need to learn and remember for A-Level Economics. Think of the time you spend studying as an investment with great potential profits at the end of the course.

## Distinguish Between Microeconomics and Macroeconomics

1) Every topic you cover during the course will fall under either microeconomics (which looks at individuals, firms and markets), or macroeconomics (which looks at the economy as a whole). In the exams, there'll be a paper for each of these and a third paper which tests a mixture of the two.

2) Organise your notes into these two areas so that you can be confident of the differences between them before revising.

3) There are also links between microeconomics and macroeconomics that you need to be aware of. Every time you study a new topic, make a note of any links you find between the two. This will help you to understand how different elements of economic theory are connected, giving you a clearer understanding of the subject.

Tiff was a fan of microeconomics — it had helped her to buy a whole house for only £9.99.

## Recognise the Two Kinds of Economic Statement

Throughout your course, you need to be able to recognise the two main types of economic statement:

### Positive Statements

• These are objective statements which you can test against the available evidence, e.g. "A reduction in the supply of oil will lead to increasing oil prices."

• They're important because they can be tested to show whether or not economic ideas are correct.

### Normative Statements

• These are subjective statements — they're opinions which can't be tested, only agreed or disagreed with. E.g. "The minimum wage should be increased to £15 an hour."

• They're important because they can influence decision-making and government policy.

## Understand the Wider Context

1) Learn about economics in the real world by watching the news or by reading articles in the economics and business sections of websites and newspapers. This will help you to understand the relevance of the concepts and theories you're studying in class.

2) Practise analysing economics news to prepare for exam questions that involve case studies or extracts. For example, you could try writing explanations for new economic policies or predicting the effects that environmental events might have on various economies.

# Economics

## Get Familiar With Graphs and Diagrams

1) <u>Graphs</u> and <u>diagrams</u> help you to <u>visualise difficult concepts</u> and <u>present your analysis</u> more clearly.

2) <u>Practise</u> drawing and labelling them throughout the course so you can produce them <u>quickly</u> and <u>confidently</u> if you need to in an exam.

3) Make sure you practise <u>reading</u> and <u>interpreting</u> graphs and diagrams too. In the exams, you may have to pick out <u>relevant information</u> from a graph or diagram and use your own knowledge to <u>analyse</u> its significance.

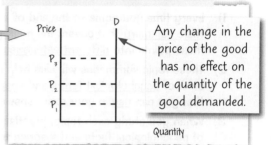

EXAMPLE:

Here's a graph you could draw to show perfectly inelastic demand.

Any change in the price of the good has no effect on the quantity of the good demanded.

## Practise Your Maths Skills

1) You might have to do some calculations in the exams. Memorise the formulas you'll need (e.g. by using flash cards) and practise them regularly before the exams so that you can quickly identify which calculation you need and how to perform it.

2) Show your working out when you do any calculations in the exams, including any formula you've used — you might still get marks for working even if your final answer is wrong.

Agnieszka enjoyed performing calculations in front of an audience.

## Learn How to Tackle Extended-Answer Questions

1) When writing extended answers, make sure you demonstrate <u>all the skills</u> you're being tested on.

2) For example, if you're asked to <u>evaluate the extent</u> to which increasing the National Minimum Wage (NMW) in the UK can help to correct labour market failure, you'd need to:

- <u>Define</u> NMW and labour market failure to earn <u>AO1</u> marks.
- <u>Explain</u> how the NMW affects the labour market for <u>AO2</u> marks.
- Discuss the <u>advantages</u> and <u>disadvantages</u> of an NMW increase for <u>AO3</u> marks.
- <u>Weigh up</u> both sides of the argument and <u>make your own judgement</u> about how successful an NMW increase could be to correct labour market failure in the UK to get <u>AO4</u> marks.

---

## There could be an economics pun here, but there's not enough demand...

There are plenty of new definitions to learn in A-Level Economics, and they're a really useful way of gaining easy marks in the exam. They can be used in most of your answers, so make sure you include them in your revision.

# Psychology

A-Level Psychology gets you thinking about lots of things, such as how memory works, why we have phobias and how you're supposed to pass those pesky exams. These next pages should help with that last bit.

## Summarise Topics While You Study

1) Every time you come to the end of a new topic in class, write a topic summary that covers the main points — you could organise these points into different categories so they're easier to learn.

2) These topic summaries will also help you to create a bank of psychological terms and specialist vocabulary that you can use in your exam answers.

3) When you study each topic, practise applying your knowledge of psychological facts and theories to different contexts, e.g. if you're studying eyewitness testimony, you could read news articles and think about what might have affected the testimony in them. This will help you to prepare for exam questions that require you to explain unseen scenarios.

> Topic Summary
>
> • Theories and concepts
>
> • Specialist terminology
>
> • Research and studies
>
> • Points of evaluation, e.g. of studies, theories or research methods

## Know Your Psychological Studies

1) Whenever you learn a new psychological study, condense your notes for it down to the key information that you need for the exam — include the name of the psychologist(s), the topic of the study, the method, results, conclusions and some evaluation (e.g. if there were any ethical or ecological issues with the research methods).

**EXAMPLE:**

Here's the beginning of some condensed notes on a key study about eyewitness testimony.

> ### Loftus and Palmer (1974) — Eyewitness Testimony
>
> Experiment 1 — Method
>
> • Participants shown film of multiple-car crash. Asked questions, e.g. "How fast do you think the cars were going when they hit?"
>
> • In different conditions, the word 'hit' was replaced with 'smashed', 'collided', 'bumped' or 'contacted'.
>
> Experiment 1 — Results
>
> • Participants given the word 'smashed' estimated the highest speed (an average of 41 mph).
>
> • Those given the word 'contacted' gave the lowest estimate (an average of 32 mph).

2) Make sure you can use this information in different ways — extended-answer questions will require you to discuss studies in depth, but including them in shorter responses can also strengthen your answers.

# Psychology

## Get to Grips with Research Methods

1) Get familiar with the main types of <u>research method</u> (e.g. <u>experiments</u>, <u>observation</u> and <u>interviews</u>) and <u>scientific processes</u> used in <u>psychological experiments</u>, as well as the <u>data handling</u> and <u>analysis techniques</u> they use.

2) Learn the <u>pros</u> and <u>cons</u> of different methods of <u>research</u> and <u>analysis</u> so you can use them to help you <u>evaluate</u> different studies. Evaluating studies will be helpful for a range of questions, not just ones specifically about research methods.

3) When you learn about a new research method, consider whether issues such as <u>ethics</u>, <u>bias</u>, and <u>social sensitivity</u> are relevant to the study. Thinking about the <u>wider issues</u> of each study as you learn it will get you into the habit of evaluating studies for the exam.

4) In the exam, you could be asked to <u>design</u> your own psychological procedures or to <u>make suggestions</u> for how to improve a study, so knowing these points of evaluation will help you to prepare.

Okeyo's covert observational techniques left a lot of room for improvement.

## Get to Know the Different Kinds of Exam Questions

1) <u>Read the front of each exam paper</u> carefully — some of the questions will be <u>compulsory</u>, but there are some papers where you'll have to <u>pick a topic</u> from a selection. <u>Only answer what you need to</u>.

2) <u>Use the information</u> given in each question to help you answer, especially if you're given some <u>data</u> to analyse or <u>bullet points</u> of what to include.

3) Check to find out what <u>question types</u> you'll have to answer in the exams. These are some of the main types of question you might have to tackle:

### Multiple-Choice Questions

Check the <u>question wording</u> carefully so you don't make simple mistakes. Some questions might ask for <u>two answers</u>, or ask you to <u>find the wrong answer</u>.

### Scenario Questions

These questions ask you to <u>use</u> your <u>psychology knowledge</u> to explain a <u>hypothetical situation</u>, e.g. to explain, using your knowledge of conditioning, how a student could be encouraged to revise for an exam.

### Data-Response Questions

These questions test your awareness of <u>data handling</u> and <u>analysis techniques</u>. Practise by <u>interpreting sets of data</u> and <u>doing calculations</u> and <u>statistical tests</u>.

### Extended-Answer Questions

Make a <u>quick plan</u> for these questions. If you get an 'evaluate' or 'discuss' question, it's especially important to demonstrate your <u>evaluation skills</u> rather than just <u>presenting facts</u>.

---

## Psychologists have the softest hair — they spend all their time conditioning...

Try to get into the habit of going over material regularly during the course — this will help you get familiar with the psychological studies, research methods and terminology so you can refer to them confidently in the exams.

# Sociology

Sociology is all about studying society and understanding things like culture, identity and power — which, incidentally, is what I named my latest band.  Here are some handy ways to help you succeed in the subject.

## Create Your Own Bank of Information

Use these <u>methods</u> to help you <u>learn information</u> as you go through the course:

> **Make cue cards**
>
> Create cue cards with information about the <u>key studies</u>, <u>theories</u> and <u>concepts</u> within each topic — for each study, write down which <u>topics</u> it relates to and any <u>key findings and vital criticisms</u>.

> **Note similarities and differences between studies**
>
> Keep a record of the <u>links</u> between different <u>topics and studies</u> — this will help you get used to drawing on relevant examples from <u>across the course</u> when writing <u>essay-style answers</u>.

> **Create a glossary of terms and concepts**
>
> This will help you to <u>understand key ideas</u> and give you a bank of <u>concise explanations</u> you can use in the exam.

> **Learn all the different research methods**
>
> Make sure you know the <u>suitability</u> of research methods in <u>different circumstances</u> — note down <u>example studies</u> of when each method was used so you can use these in the exam.

**EXAMPLE:**

### Milgram (1974) — Ethical Issues

- Obedience experiment — volunteers gave someone (an actor) electric shocks for incorrect answers in a memory test, but weren't aware that the shocks were being faked by the actor.
- Results showed how people can obey authority without question — shows how ordinary people could take part in war crimes or genocide.
- Criticised for deceiving participants — they didn't know the real purpose of the study. Potential psychological harm to participants.

## Do Some Further Sociology Research

You should take some time to <u>research topics you've covered</u> to <u>improve your understanding</u> of sociology.

1) Start with areas you <u>find interesting</u> and <u>want to know more</u> about.  Keep a note of <u>how your research relates</u> to the topics you've covered in class.

2) If you have a <u>different opinion</u> on theories you've learnt about in class, see if there are studies that <u>offer alternative perspectives</u>.

3) Stay <u>up to date with the news</u>.  In the exams, talking about <u>new legislation</u> or <u>studies</u> in relation to traditional sociological theories can help <u>demonstrate your understanding</u> of the subject.

4) If you're unsure of any <u>concepts</u> or <u>theories</u>, <u>research</u> them further or <u>ask your teacher</u> about them — sociology is full of complex ideas, so it's important to <u>make sure you understand everything</u> when you're revising.

Olivia was sure that dressing up for high society portraits counted as research.

# Sociology

## Prepare for Different Exam Questions

1) Make sure you're familiar with the <u>format</u> of each exam paper — the papers might contain <u>compulsory</u> questions, <u>non-compulsory</u> questions (where you have to pick which questions to answer), or a <u>mixture</u> of the two.

2) Practise answering the <u>different types of question</u> that you'll see in the exam:

<u>Short-answer questions</u> test your <u>knowledge</u> and <u>application</u> of it — practise writing <u>concise answers</u> and <u>explanations</u> for these.

Long-answer questions will require some <u>planning</u>. You'll need to <u>acknowledge different perspectives</u> and use appropriate <u>evidence</u> to <u>weigh up ideas</u> before coming to a <u>conclusion</u>. You'll need to apply your sociology knowledge and draw upon relevant <u>sociological theories</u> and <u>concepts</u> to support your answer.

3) Aim to <u>be specific</u> in all of your answers and <u>define</u> sociological terms <u>clearly</u>.

4) Show your knowledge of <u>theories</u>, <u>concepts</u>, <u>evidence</u> and <u>research methods</u>, and make sure you <u>develop</u> your answers by showing how this sociology knowledge <u>relates to the question</u>.

## Use the Materials You're Given in the Exam

1) For some exam questions, you'll be given a <u>short text</u>, <u>source</u> or <u>data set</u> to read and analyse.

2) Make sure that you <u>use the most relevant points</u> from this material in your answers — the information is there to give you <u>hints</u> on what you could write about, and you need to <u>explicitly reference</u> it in your answers.

3) <u>Build on</u> the material by linking it to <u>relevant sociological theories</u> and your <u>own understanding</u> — this will show that you can <u>apply your knowledge</u>.

4) In some longer essay-style questions, you may need to <u>critically evaluate</u> the material provided.

I think I prefer the silk...

## You don't need to be called Karl to get top Marx...

Make sure that you understand the sociological studies, theories and concepts that you cover during the course. This will give you the core knowledge you need to build on when you're asked to evaluate things in the exam.

# Extended Project Qualification

You might not have heard of the Extended Project Qualification (EPQ), but it's a great chance to learn more about something that really interests you — this is because you get to choose what your project is about.

## You Can Complete an EPQ Alongside Your A-Levels

1) The EPQ requires you to <u>plan</u>, <u>research</u> and <u>complete</u> a fairly lengthy project.

2) You get to choose which of these forms your project will take:

   - A 5000-word <u>essay</u> or <u>report</u>
   - An <u>artefact</u>, e.g. a piece of artwork or a game, and a written report (usually around 1000 words long)
   - A <u>production</u> or <u>performance</u>, e.g. producing a play, and a written report (usually around 1000 words long)

Antoni was sure his attempt to become an artefact would lead to an interesting EPQ report.

3) You also get to <u>choose</u> what your project is about — it might be <u>related</u> to something <u>academic</u> or to a <u>potential career</u>, but it's also a chance to explore <u>something new</u>. The key is to choose a topic that <u>excites you</u>, but you'll need to <u>check with your supervisor</u> whether it's <u>suitable</u>.

4) As part of the EPQ, you have to <u>produce a log</u> (to keep a record of your progress and why you made certain decisions) and <u>give a presentation</u> (see the next page).

5) The project helps you to <u>develop a range of skills</u>, including your time management, research, organisation and critical thinking skills. You'll be marked on things like <u>project management</u>, <u>research</u> and <u>evaluation</u>.

*The EPQ takes a substantial amount of time to complete (around 120 hours), so think about whether you can manage the extra workload.*

## Break Your Project Up into Stages

1) Dividing your project into <u>manageable chunks</u> will make the work seem less daunting.

2) <u>Write a list</u> of everything you'll need to do and set <u>rough deadlines</u> for when you want to have achieved certain parts of your project, e.g. finishing your research or writing a first draft.

3) You'll spend plenty of time <u>researching</u> your chosen topic, but you don't have to do it all in one go. In fact, <u>researching in smaller chunks</u> can often be quite helpful — you can do some <u>initial research</u>, see what you learn from it and then use this to <u>choose new areas</u> to focus on (see pages 22-23 for more on how to do research).

4) You'll probably want to <u>write</u> your <u>essay</u> or <u>report in chunks</u> too. This will help you to complete it around your other studies, and make the idea of writing a longer piece of work feel less daunting (there's more about essay writing on pages 18-21).

5) Find out what EPQ <u>support</u> is available at your school or college — some might offer <u>workshops</u> for <u>different stages</u> of the process.

# Extended Project Qualification

## Prepare for Your Presentation

1) Your presentation should have a <u>clear structure</u> and cover a few things:
   - What your project is <u>about</u> and how you <u>developed</u> it
   - How you <u>researched</u> your project (e.g. what <u>sources</u> you used)
   - What you <u>found</u> from completing your project
   - What <u>went well</u> and what you could have <u>improved on</u>

2) Even if you've given a presentation before, spend some time <u>preparing</u> for it:

People always wanted to talk to Ethel about her unique style of presentation..

### Work on Your Presentation Skills

- Make a few <u>bullet-pointed cue cards</u> that you can use as <u>prompts</u> while you talk — it's better to use prompts like these rather than just reading from a piece of paper or a screen.
- Consider whether you want to use a <u>visual aid</u>, e.g. a projected presentation, to help illustrate your points.
- <u>Practise</u> giving your presentation to friends and family — this will make you feel <u>more comfortable</u> speaking to people about the project and will help you to see <u>how long</u> your presentation is.
- <u>Speak clearly</u> and try to <u>enjoy</u> the chance to share a topic you're passionate about.

3) There will be time for people to ask <u>questions</u> after your presentation — you might find it useful to <u>prepare some answers</u> to potential questions before the day.

## The EPQ is Popular with Universities

1) As the EPQ develops a lot of <u>skills</u> that are important at university and shows that you have an <u>interest</u> in exploring a subject further, it can <u>enhance</u> your university application and make you <u>stand out</u>.

2) An EPQ is worth <u>UCAS Tariff points</u>, so completing one might help you to meet your university offer if it's based on this points system.

3) Some universities will even make <u>adjusted offers</u>, e.g. an offer with <u>lower grade requirements</u>, for students who complete an EPQ.

4) Even if you don't plan on going to university, it'll still be a <u>valuable addition</u> to your CV because the skills you gain will be useful in the workplace too.

Ralph wasn't expecting his EPQ to have such a positive effect on his popularity.

## My extended project involved an awful lot of elastic bands...

Try to be flexible while you're doing your EPQ. Use your initial research to give you direction, but be prepared to adjust your project as you go to get the most out of it — reassessing your work is a natural part of the process.

# Extended Picnic Qualification

Despite its name, the Extended Picnic Qualification (not to be confused with the other EPQ, of course) is no picnic... But don't worry if you're finding it tough — this page should give you some food for thought.

## Aim to Make Your Picnic As Long As Possible

1) Remember that it's called the <u>Extended</u> Picnic Qualification for a reason — check with your teacher about the ~~cheese~~ exam board requirements, but you'll need to host your picnic for <u>at least 3 days</u>.

2) To avoid things quickly going <u>pear-shaped</u>, it's important to <u>check the weather</u> before you go. You don't want to get <u>five minutes</u> in only to find yourself stuck with a basket full of <u>sodden sandwiches</u> and a raincoat that really doesn't <u>cut the mustard</u>.

> If you're worried about <u>getting in a pickle</u> with the weather, you could always host your picnic in <u>a sunnier country</u>. You can apply to the British Association of Picnickers (<u>BAP</u>) for funding.

## Choose Your Companions Wisely

A good picnic is all about <u>the company</u>, so <u>choose carefully</u>. Here are some <u>potential candidates</u>:

- <u>A teddy bear</u> — a <u>traditional</u> choice for a picnic, but a <u>strong</u> one. It may be unlikely to provide <u>stimulating conversation</u>, but it will probably leave you <u>most of the food</u>.
- <u>A personal chef</u> — this is <u>frowned upon</u> by some teachers, but <u>isn't strictly cheating</u>.
- <u>Someone called Nick</u> — you'll definitely want to <u>pick</u> them.

> Pick me — alpaca 'nuff food for both of us!

## Bring Enough Food and Drink

When it comes to the EPQ, this is the real <u>bread and butter stuff</u>:

<u>Rock and roll</u>

<u>A piece of cake</u> — this one should be <u>easy</u> to remember.

<u>Sandwiches</u> — with these, it's much better to have <u>one too many</u> than to find yourself <u>one short</u>.

<u>Eggs</u> — split between <u>several baskets</u> if possible.

<u>Lemonade</u> — if life gives you lemons, you'll have <u>bottomless refills</u>.

---

## With the right planning, hosting your picnic should be a walk in the park...

You're not out of the woods (figuratively speaking) once you've finished your picnic — you'll have to complete a post-project assessment (updating your social media) and then some post-project analysis (eating up the leftovers).

# Before the Exam

Hopefully by the time an exam comes around, you'll be feeling fairly comfortable with your knowledge and exam technique, but it can still be nerve-wracking. Here are some tips to help you get in the zone.

## Get Your Things Together the Night Before

Your focus the night before should be on practical preparations instead of last-minute revision:

1) Pack your bag with anything you need to take into the exam — don't forget spare pens.
2) Make sure you know where and when the exam is.
3) Try to do something that takes your mind off the exam, e.g exercising or watching TV.
4) Read over some notes if it's helpful, but don't try to learn anything new.
5) Eat a balanced meal and try your best to get a good night's sleep (see page 37).

## Make a Routine for Exam Days

Sticking to a routine can help to make things feel more comfortable and familiar. You could try:

Setting an alarm so that you wake up with plenty of time to get ready.

Choosing something comfortable to wear (if you don't have to wear a uniform).

Eating a healthy breakfast. Don't worry too much if you don't manage a big breakfast because of nerves — you can still do well in the exam.

Looking over key bits of information (e.g. definitions, formulas, etc.) if you find it helpful, but don't do too much.

Making sure you leave home with plenty of time to get to the exam, especially if you need to use public transport. Try not to get there too early though, especially if a longer wait might make you feel more nervous.

## Try to Stay Calm When You Arrive

1) Avoid talking about the exam while you wait. It might help to chat about something else or to move away from others if you need some space to mentally prepare yourself.

2) Don't worry about topics you wish you'd spent more time on — focus on the information you do know.

3) If you find yourself panicking, try to focus on your breathing. Taking some deep breaths can help to calm you down and distract you from your nerves before you go into the exam.

Mikaela was a pro at staying calm under pressure.

---

### I did some yoga while I ate my breakfast — it was a balanced meal...

Try not to worry if you can't stick to your pre-exam routine for a particular reason — it's there to help you feel more comfortable and reduce your nerves, but it's the study and revision you've done that will help you succeed.

68

# During the Exam

Once you get into the exam and sit down at your desk, it's your time to shine. Personally, I like to wear a T-shirt that's covered in flashing lights for that purpose — anyway, onto the exam itself...

## Don't Panic During the Exam

It's important to <u>stay focused</u> during the exam and to <u>make the most</u> of the <u>time</u> you have.

 **A-Level Exam Success Paper 1**

- When you sit down, <u>lay out your stationery</u> to help you get into the <u>right mindset</u>. Then, once you're allowed, <u>read</u> through the instructions <u>carefully</u>.

- Make sure that you <u>only answer</u> the questions <u>you need to</u>.

- To help you <u>understand difficult questions</u>, you could highlight <u>command words</u> or <u>key concepts</u> in the question wording.

- Keep an eye on the <u>clock</u> to help you <u>manage your time</u> — this will mean you're more likely to have <u>time to answer</u> everything and <u>check</u> your work.

- Look at <u>how many marks</u> a question is worth when deciding <u>how long to spend</u> on it — try to <u>avoid</u> spending too much time on questions that aren't worth many marks.

- Put a <u>quick plan</u> together for any longer answers, e.g. <u>essays</u>.

## If you find yourself panicking...

- Take some <u>deep breaths</u> and drink a few <u>sips of water</u> — this can help you refocus on the exam.

- If you're stuck on a question, <u>move on</u> to the next question and <u>come back</u> to it later.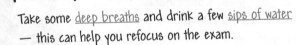

- Concentrate on <u>what you can do</u>, not what you can't. Don't get distracted by other people if they seem to be ahead.

# After the Exam

No matter how you think an exam went, celebrate getting another one out of the way and have a little break once it's over — each one you finish is a paving stone on your path to post-exam freedom.

## Don't Worry About the Exam

1) Worrying <u>won't change</u> anything, so <u>don't</u> spend too much time <u>thinking</u> or <u>talking</u> about the exam once it's over.

2) It can be helpful to think about whether there's anything <u>you could do better</u> next time though:

Jenny's brother taught her his favourite method for putting things out of his mind.

- If you <u>ran out of time</u>, consider how you might use your time <u>more effectively</u> in the next exam.

- If you <u>felt tired</u>, look at whether you could <u>improve</u> your routine <u>the night before</u>.

- If you <u>panicked</u>, try practising some <u>relaxation techniques</u> you can use to <u>stay calm</u> in future exams.

## Try to Relax After the Exam

1) <u>Recharge</u> by doing something you <u>enjoy</u> or <u>find relaxing</u> — this could be something as simple as going for a walk or watching a film.

2) If you have another exam <u>the same day</u> or <u>the next day</u>, make sure that you still <u>take a break</u> before you start your <u>final exam preparations</u> (see p.67).

3) When you've had a break, <u>put your notes</u> for the exam you've done <u>away</u> — this can act as a physical reminder of <u>what you've achieved already</u>.

## Celebrate Finishing Your Exams

1) Once you've finished <u>all your exams</u>, put your notes and revision materials <u>out of sight</u> (but don't throw any of them away) and give yourself a break from thinking about exams.

2) Plan a <u>treat</u> to <u>celebrate</u> all the hard work you've done in the last couple of years.

---

**My final exam was about astrophysics — I was over the moon when it was done...**

If you're worried that an exam went really badly, try to remember that you can't be sure what mark you've got and it's better to focus on your next exam instead.  You could also talk to a teacher or parent for reassurance.

# Making a Timetable

You may have made a revision timetable at GCSE, but in case you need reminding, here's how it's done...

Your revision planner and timetable can be found on pages 74-97. There are spaces for you to fill in your exams, other commitments and planned revision sessions.

## Write Down the Dates of Your Exams

1) The first step is to find out when your exams are and fill in the exam timetable on page 74.

2) Refer to this regularly to keep track of when your exams are and to help you stay focused on your priorities.

EXAMPLE:

### Exam Timetable

| Subject | Paper | Date | Time |
|---|---|---|---|
| English Lit | Paper 1: Drama | May 12th (Wed) | 09:00 |
| Maths | Pure Maths 1 | May 19th (Wed) | 14:00 |
| Maths | Pure Maths 2 | May 21st (Fri) | 09:00 |
| Physics | Paper 1 | May 24th (Mon) | 09:00 |

Hilda had plenty of time, but she was desperate for a table to put it all down on.

## Break Each Subject Down Into Topics

Fill in the topic planners for each of your subjects — they're on pages 75-79:

1) Look at the exam board specification for each subject to find a list of topics, or ask your teachers. For subjects that have very large topics, break each topic down into smaller sub-topics.

2) Put a tick in the correct column to show how confident you feel with each topic.

3) You can update the topic planners as you revise so that you can see your progress.

EXAMPLE:

### Topic Planner — Subject: _____Maths_____

| Topic | ☹ | 😐 | 😊 |
|---|---|---|---|
| Proofs | ✓ | | |
| Algebra | ✓ | ✓ | ✓ |
| Trigonometry | ✓ | | |
| Differentiation | ✓ | ✓ | |

This isn't the only way of tracking your revision progress — you can adapt this system depending on what works best for you.

# Making a Timetable

## Begin Filling in Your Revision Timetable

1) Write down all of your <u>exams</u> in the correct days of the <u>timetable</u>.

2) Start from the <u>end</u> — write down your <u>last exam</u> on the <u>last page</u> of the timetable, then <u>work backwards</u>, adding in the dates of your other exams.

**EXAMPLE:**

Say your last exam is English Lit Paper 3 on the morning of Tuesday 22nd June, you would:

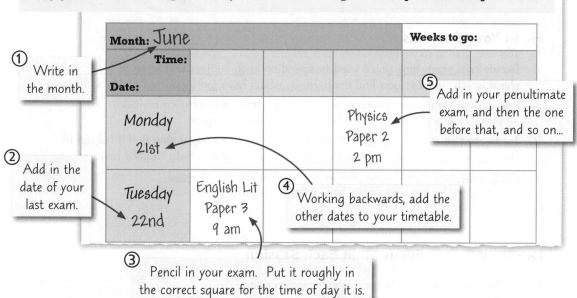

① Write in the month.

② Add in the date of your last exam.

③ Pencil in your exam. Put it roughly in the correct square for the time of day it is.

④ Working backwards, add the other dates to your timetable.

⑤ Add in your penultimate exam, and then the one before that, and so on...

| Month: June | Time: | | | Weeks to go: |
|---|---|---|---|---|
| Date: | | | | |
| Monday 21st | | | Physics Paper 2 2 pm | |
| Tuesday 22nd | English Lit Paper 3 9 am | | | |

## Fill in the Times You're Going to Revise

1) The revision timetable in this book has been split into <u>five sessions</u> — the <u>time spaces</u> have been left blank so that you can <u>choose them yourself</u>.

2) To help you <u>divide your day</u> into revision sessions, think about:

- what <u>time</u> of day you <u>work best</u>
- when you <u>get up</u> and <u>go to bed</u>
- <u>how long</u> you'll <u>revise</u> each day
- fitting in <u>sensible breaks</u>

A good rule of thumb is to take a <u>10-minute break every hour</u> — you could split this into two 5-minute breaks.

3) It's <u>up to you how long</u> each session is.

4) You <u>don't need</u> to use <u>every session each day</u> — you can leave some sessions blank if you don't plan to be revising then, or if you still have lessons at school or college. <u>Adapt</u> your revision timetable to your circumstances.

# Making a Timetable

## Add Your Hobbies and Commitments

1) It's important to leave some time for your other commitments. If you overload yourself, revision might become more stressful and you won't be as productive (see p.36-37 for advice on this).

2) Go through your revision timetable and add in time for things like hobbies and exercise, holidays and birthdays, part-time jobs and time with friends and family.

Jackie was as committed to her timetable as she was to her turntable.

## Fill in Your Subjects

1) Decide how much time you'll need to spend on each subject and when to start revising it by thinking about which subjects you find the hardest, which have more content and which exams come first.

2) Add your subjects into the timetable (from the first week of your revision) — make sure you allow enough time to revise every subject.

3) Try to revise a mix of different subjects every day. You might also find it helpful to revise your subjects in a different order each day to add variety to your revision.

4) Keep some time free in your plan in case something unexpected comes up — having a few gaps will make it easy to adapt.

## Decide What to Focus on in Each Session

Next, think about what you'll spend each session doing. You could focus on a topic or dedicate time to an activity.

You don't have to decide what to do for all of your sessions immediately — you might prefer to do this at the start of each week.

### TOPICS

- For each subject, look at your topic planner and think about which topics you should prioritise. You'll need to make sure every topic is covered somewhere though.

- Aim to include topics multiple times so you can revise them thoroughly.

- Leave a gap before revisiting a topic to help the information sink in better.

- Don't finish with a topic too soon before your exam or you might forget things.

### ACTIVITIES

- You might find it better to focus some sessions on activities rather than topics. E.g. you could make a mind map to compare different texts for English Literature.

- As the exams get nearer, you'll also want to spend some sessions doing past papers and timed essays to help you practise for the exam.

# Making a Timetable

## Marvel at Your Completed Revision Timetable

EXAMPLE:

This timetable uses <u>50-minute</u> revision <u>sessions</u>, with <u>10-minute breaks</u> after each one.

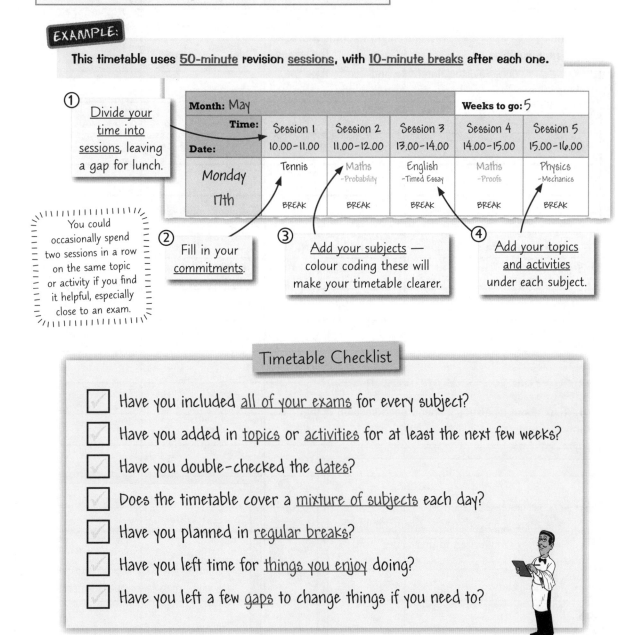

① <u>Divide your time into sessions</u>, leaving a gap for lunch.

You could occasionally spend two sessions in a row on the same topic or activity if you find it helpful, especially close to an exam.

| Month: May | | | | | Weeks to go: 5 |
|---|---|---|---|---|---|
| **Time:** / **Date:** | Session 1 10.00–11.00 | Session 2 11.00–12.00 | Session 3 13.00–14.00 | Session 4 14.00–15.00 | Session 5 15.00–16.00 |
| Monday 17th | Tennis BREAK | Maths –Probability BREAK | English –Timed Essay BREAK | Maths –Proofs BREAK | Physics –Mechanics BREAK |

② Fill in your <u>commitments</u>.

③ <u>Add your subjects</u> — colour coding these will make your timetable clearer.

④ <u>Add your topics and activities</u> under each subject.

### Timetable Checklist

☑ Have you included <u>all of your exams</u> for every subject?

☑ Have you added in <u>topics</u> or <u>activities</u> for at least the next few weeks?

☑ Have you double-checked the <u>dates</u>?

☑ Does the timetable cover a <u>mixture of subjects</u> each day?

☑ Have you planned in <u>regular breaks</u>?

☑ Have you left time for <u>things you enjoy</u> doing?

☑ Have you left a few <u>gaps</u> to change things if you need to?

## I turned my timetable into a paper aeroplane — time started to fly by...

It's best to try and stick to your timetable, but it's okay to adapt it as you go along. For example, if something doesn't go to plan one day, just fit any missed revision into the gaps you've left in the timetable and carry on.

# Exam Timetable

| Subject | Paper | Date | Time |
|---------|-------|------|------|
|         |       |      |      |
|         |       |      |      |
|         |       |      |      |
|         |       |      |      |
|         |       |      |      |
|         |       |      |      |
|         |       |      |      |
|         |       |      |      |
|         |       |      |      |
|         |       |      |      |
|         |       |      |      |
|         |       |      |      |
|         |       |      |      |
|         |       |      |      |
|         |       |      |      |
|         |       |      |      |
|         |       |      |      |
|         |       |      |      |
|         |       |      |      |
|         |       |      |      |
|         |       |      |      |
|         |       |      |      |
|         |       |      |      |
|         |       |      |      |

# Topic Planner — Subject: _____

| Topic | ☹ | ☺ | 😉 |
|---|---|---|---|
|  |  |  |  |
|  |  |  |  |
|  |  |  |  |
|  |  |  |  |
|  |  |  |  |
|  |  |  |  |
|  |  |  |  |
|  |  |  |  |
|  |  |  |  |
|  |  |  |  |
|  |  |  |  |
|  |  |  |  |
|  |  |  |  |
|  |  |  |  |
|  |  |  |  |
|  |  |  |  |
|  |  |  |  |
|  |  |  |  |
|  |  |  |  |
|  |  |  |  |
|  |  |  |  |
|  |  |  |  |
|  |  |  |  |
|  |  |  |  |

# Topic Planner — Subject: _____

| Topic | 😕 | 🙂 | 😉 |
|-------|-----|-----|-----|
|  |  |  |  |
|  |  |  |  |
|  |  |  |  |
|  |  |  |  |
|  |  |  |  |
|  |  |  |  |
|  |  |  |  |
|  |  |  |  |
|  |  |  |  |
|  |  |  |  |
|  |  |  |  |
|  |  |  |  |
|  |  |  |  |
|  |  |  |  |
|  |  |  |  |
|  |  |  |  |
|  |  |  |  |
|  |  |  |  |
|  |  |  |  |
|  |  |  |  |
|  |  |  |  |
|  |  |  |  |
|  |  |  |  |

# Topic Planner — Subject: _____

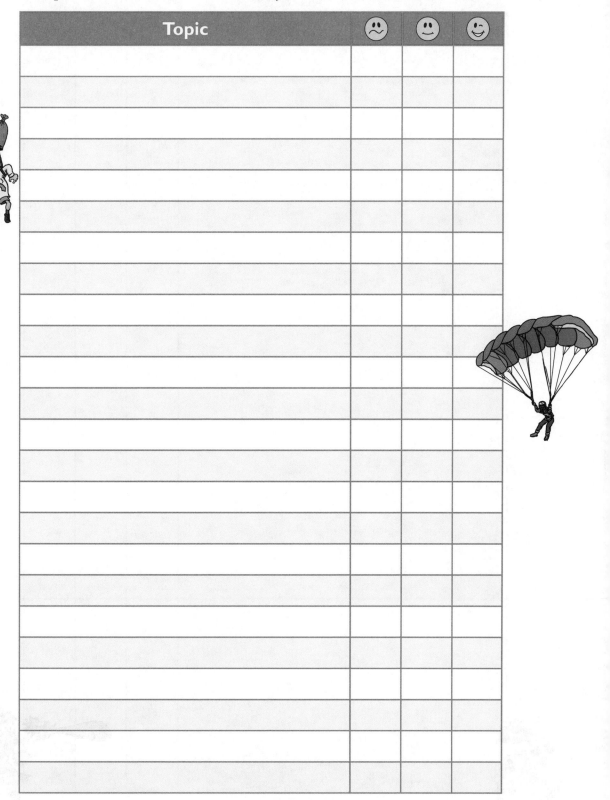

| Topic | 😠 | 😐 | 😊 |
|---|---|---|---|
| | | | |
| | | | |
| | | | |
| | | | |
| | | | |
| | | | |
| | | | |
| | | | |
| | | | |
| | | | |
| | | | |
| | | | |
| | | | |
| | | | |
| | | | |
| | | | |
| | | | |
| | | | |
| | | | |
| | | | |
| | | | |
| | | | |
| | | | |
| | | | |

# Topic Planner — Subject: _____

| Topic | 🙁 | 🙂 | 😉 |
|---|---|---|---|
| | | | |
| | | | |
| | | | |
| | | | |
| | | | |
| | | | |
| | | | |
| | | | |
| | | | |
| | | | |
| | | | |
| | | | |
| | | | |
| | | | |
| | | | |
| | | | |
| | | | |
| | | | |
| | | | |
| | | | |
| | | | |

# Topic Planner — Subject: _____

| Topic | 🙁 | 🙂 | 😊 |
|-------|----|----|----|
|  |  |  |  |
|  |  |  |  |
|  |  |  |  |
|  |  |  |  |
|  |  |  |  |
|  |  |  |  |
|  |  |  |  |
|  |  |  |  |
|  |  |  |  |
|  |  |  |  |
|  |  |  |  |
|  |  |  |  |
|  |  |  |  |
|  |  |  |  |
|  |  |  |  |
|  |  |  |  |
|  |  |  |  |
|  |  |  |  |
|  |  |  |  |
|  |  |  |  |
|  |  |  |  |
|  |  |  |  |
|  |  |  |  |
|  |  |  |  |

# Revision Timetable

You can find an online version of the timetable at cgpbooks.co.uk/ALevelTimetable.

| Month: | | | | Weeks to go: | |
|---|---|---|---|---|---|
| Time: / Date: | | | | | |
| Monday | | | | | |
| Tuesday | | | | | |
| Wednesday | | | | | |
| Thursday | | | | | |
| Friday | | | | | |
| Saturday | | | | | |
| Sunday | | | | | |

# Revision Timetable

| Month: | | | | Weeks to go: | |
|---|---|---|---|---|---|
| Time: <br> Date: | | | | | |
| Monday | | | | | |
| Tuesday | | | | | |
| Wednesday | | | | | |
| Thursday | | | | | |
| Friday | | | | | |
| Saturday | | | | | |
| Sunday | | | | | |

# Revision Timetable

| Month: | | | | Weeks to go: | |
|---|---|---|---|---|---|
| Time:<br>Date: | | | | | |
| Monday | | | | | |
| Tuesday | | | | | |
| Wednesday | | | | | |
| Thursday | | | | | |
| Friday | | | | | |
| Saturday | | | | | |
| Sunday | | | | | |

# Revision Timetable

| Month: | | | | Weeks to go: | |
|---|---|---|---|---|---|
| Time: / Date: | | | | | |
| Monday | | | | | |
| Tuesday | | | | | |
| Wednesday | | | | | |
| Thursday | | | | | |
| Friday | | | | | |
| Saturday | | | | | |
| Sunday | | | | | |

# Revision Timetable

| Month: | | | | Weeks to go: | |
|---|---|---|---|---|---|
| Time: / Date: | | | | | |
| Monday | | | | | |
| Tuesday | | | | | |
| Wednesday | | | | | |
| Thursday | | | | | |
| Friday | | | | | |
| Saturday | | | | | |
| Sunday | | | | | |

Your Revision Timetable

# Revision Timetable

| Month: | | | | Weeks to go: | |
|---|---|---|---|---|---|
| Time: / Date: | | | | | |
| Monday | | | | | |
| Tuesday | | | | | |
| Wednesday | | | | | |
| Thursday | | | | | |
| Friday | | | | | |
| Saturday | | | | | |
| Sunday | | | | | |

# Revision Timetable

| Month: | | | | Weeks to go: | |
|---|---|---|---|---|---|
| Time: / Date: | | | | | |
| Monday | | | | | |
| Tuesday | | | | | |
| Wednesday | | | | | |
| Thursday | | | | | |
| Friday | | | | | |
| Saturday | | | | | |
| Sunday | | | | | |

# Revision Timetable

| Month: | | | | Weeks to go: | |
|---|---|---|---|---|---|
| **Time:**<br>**Date:** | | | | | |
| Monday | | | | | |
| Tuesday | | | | | |
| Wednesday | | | | | |
| Thursday | | | | | |
| Friday | | | | | |
| Saturday | | | | | |
| Sunday | | | | | |

# Revision Timetable

| Month: | | | | Weeks to go: | |
|---|---|---|---|---|---|
| **Time:** / **Date:** | | | | | |
| Monday | | | | | |
| Tuesday | | | | | |
| Wednesday | | | | | |
| Thursday | | | | | |
| Friday | | | | | |
| Saturday | | | | | |
| Sunday | | | | | |

# Revision Timetable

| Month: | | | | Weeks to go: | |
|---|---|---|---|---|---|
| Time: / Date: | | | | | |
| Monday | | | | | |
| Tuesday | | | | | |
| Wednesday | | | | | |
| Thursday | | | | | |
| Friday | | | | | |
| Saturday | | | | | |
| Sunday | | | | | |

# Revision Timetable

| Month: | | | | Weeks to go: | |
|---|---|---|---|---|---|
| **Time:** **Date:** | | | | | |
| Monday | | | | | |
| Tuesday | | | | | |
| Wednesday | | | | | |
| Thursday | | | | | |
| Friday | | | | | |
| Saturday | | | | | |
| Sunday | | | | | |

Your Revision Timetable

# Revision Timetable

| Month: | | | | Weeks to go: | |
|---|---|---|---|---|---|
| Time: / Date: | | | | | |
| Monday | | | | | |
| Tuesday | | | | | |
| Wednesday | | | | | |
| Thursday | | | | | |
| Friday | | | | | |
| Saturday | | | | | |
| Sunday | | | | | |

# Revision Timetable

| Month: | | | | Weeks to go: | |
|---|---|---|---|---|---|
| Time: / Date: | | | | | |
| Monday | | | | | |
| Tuesday | | | | | |
| Wednesday | | | | | |
| Thursday | | | | | |
| Friday | | | | | |
| Saturday | | | | | |
| Sunday | | | | | |

# Revision Timetable

| Month: | | | | Weeks to go: | |
|---|---|---|---|---|---|
| **Time:** / **Date:** | | | | | |
| Monday | | | | | |
| Tuesday | | | | | |
| Wednesday | | | | | |
| Thursday | | | | | |
| Friday | | | | | |
| Saturday | | | | | |
| Sunday | | | | | |

# Revision Timetable

| Month: | | | | Weeks to go: | |
|---|---|---|---|---|---|
| **Time:** / **Date:** | | | | | |
| Monday | | | | | |
| Tuesday | | | | | |
| Wednesday | | | | | |
| Thursday | | | | | |
| Friday | | | | | |
| Saturday | | | | | |
| Sunday | | | | | |

# Revision Timetable

| Month: | | | | Weeks to go: | |
|---|---|---|---|---|---|
| Time: Date: | | | | | |
| Monday | | | | | |
| Tuesday | | | | | |
| Wednesday | | | | | |
| Thursday | | | | | |
| Friday | | | | | |
| Saturday | | | | | |
| Sunday | | | | | |

# Revision Timetable

| Month: | | | | Weeks to go: | |
|---|---|---|---|---|---|
| Time: <br> Date: | | | | | |
| Monday | | | | | |
| Tuesday | | | | | |
| Wednesday | | | | | |
| Thursday | | | | | |
| Friday | | | | | |
| Saturday | | | | | |
| Sunday | | | | | |

# Revision Timetable

| Month: | | | | Weeks to go: | |
|---|---|---|---|---|---|
| Time: <br> Date: | | | | | |
| Monday | | | | | |
| Tuesday | | | | | |
| Wednesday | | | | | |
| Thursday | | | | | |
| Friday | | | | | |
| Saturday | | | | | |
| Sunday | | | | | |

# Index

# Index

# Top 10 Ultimate A-Level Tips

There's a lot to take in during your A-Levels, but here are some absolutely must-know tips for success.

- Set up an effective <u>study</u> and <u>revision space</u>.

- Use a timetable to plan your study and revision time.

- Take effective notes and file them away properly.

- Make the most of your <u>independent study time</u>.

- Read around your subjects to deepen your understanding.

- Keep your study tasks varied so you stay motivated.

- Complete <u>practice papers</u> and learn from them.

- Do your best to <u>sleep</u> and <u>eat</u> properly.

- Try to maintain a good study-life balance.

- Don't be afraid to <u>ask for help</u> — your teachers, classmates, friends and family can all <u>help you</u>.